**Receive the Empowering That Will
Launch You Into Your Destiny**

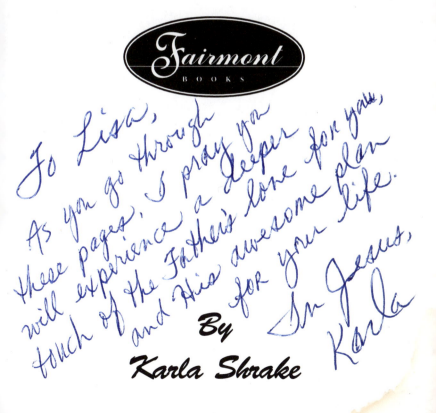

By
Karla Shrake

Mantles of Glory
Copyright © 2001 by Karla Shrake
ALL RIGHTS RESERVED

Unless otherwise noted, all Bible references are from the New American Standard Bible, copyright © 1960, 1962, 1963, 1968, 1971, 1972, 1973, 1977 by the Lockman Foundation, La Habra, California. References marked NKJ are from the New King James Version of the Bible, copyright © 1979, 1980, 1982 by Thomas Nelson, Inc., Nashville, Tennessee. References marked NIV are from the New International Version of the Bible, copyright © 1973, 1978, 1984 by International Bible Society, Colorado Springs, Colorado.

Fairmont Books is a ministry of The McDougal Foundation, Inc., a Maryland nonprofit corporation dedicated to spreading the Gospel of the Lord Jesus Christ to as many people as possible in the shortest time possible.

Published by:

Fairmont Books
P.O. Box 3595
Hagerstown, MD 21742-3595
www.mcdougalpublishing.com

ISBN 1-58158-029-0

Printed in the United States of America
For Worldwide Distribution

Dedication

To Ben, the love of my life and my husband of many years, whose patience and support enabled me to follow through on this project.

To my daughter Dawna,
the gift of my youth,
whose friendship I treasure.

To Caleb, my eldest son,
strong and devoted,
of whom I am so proud.

To my daughter Heather,
full of life and animation,
who brings me great joy.

To Jesse, my youngest son,
the gift of my older age,
my delight.

Thank you to these, my family members, who have shown such grace through not only the good times, but also through the difficult ones. I am proud to be part of such a fine team!

Acknowledgments

I would like to thank my son Caleb for the very fine illustrations he created for the book. I would also like to thank my husband Ben for the awesome book cover he designed. They are each incredibly gifted and were a delight to work with.

I would like to thank my friends Sharon Keck and Janzi Frandin, who provided vital feedback and encouragement at the onset of the project. Many thanks to my friend Sharon Vaughan for her travail in helping to birth this work. I thank my friend Kathy Brock for her faithful friendship and many prayers. And I so appreciate Jeanine Smith and Carolyn Bennett for their help in proofing — and especially for their encouragement and friendship.

I would like to thank Harold McDougal for providing a publishing company that is taking the risk to reveal the glorious things God is doing in the earth today. I am deeply grateful for McDougal Publishing, a courageous voice that is crying in the wilderness, releasing the life-giving word of the Lord to this generation.

Contents

Preface 7
Introduction 9

Part I: A New Day Dawns 13
1. The Spirit of Elijah Falls 15
2. The Curtain Is Going Up on the Final Battle 23
3. Receive Your Virility, Abraham 31
4. The True Bride Found at the Well 47
5. Journey to the Bridegroom 67
6. It's Time to Build, Warriors 87
7. And Your Whole House Shall Be Saved 109
8. Receive Your Mantle From Faith's Hall of Fame 123
9. It's Our Turn Now 143

Part II: To the Women 147
10. Jesus, the True Friend of Women 149
11. Fierce Warrior-Women 161
12. Birth Pangs, Daughters of Zion 171

Part III: To the Men 185
13. It's Your Turn 187
14. Like Father, Like Son 195
15. Time to Press 207

Part IV: To America 221
16. My Beloved America 223
17. America's Mantle of Moses 237
18. The Great Eagle Shall Rise Again 269

Preface

In *Mantles of Glory*, the author seeks to define a new era that she believes is just beginning, a time she refers to as "the day of Elijah," or "the day of restoration." She endeavors to stir the hearts of her readers, challenging them to pursue, at all costs, the greater anointing and the glory of God that is beginning to be poured out in this day. Just as Elisha pursued the mantle of Elijah, readers are exhorted to pursue their own unique mantles of destiny.

Readers are challenged to climb the mountain of God, as Moses did, and search out their own burning bushes. It is through these encounters that the Father will reveal not only Himself, but also the unique callings He has for each of His children. The Father will then open the wardrobes of Heaven, searching for just the right adornment that will empower each to fulfill his or her own destiny. May each have the grace to receive from the Father's hand his or her own personal *Mantles of Glory!*

Introduction

Many of you are no doubt familiar with the prophetic gifting and style of writing, but others may not be. An author can communicate the same message but in different ways. For instance, the author may write, "I believe the Lord is telling His people that a season of change has come," or the author may prefer to speak prophetically: " 'A season of change is upon us,' *says the Lord*." Through the inspiration of the Holy Spirit and the gift of prophecy, an author may thus communicate the Lord's mind and heart pertaining to a matter.

Although it is not my intent to do a full teaching on the prophetic gift, I do want to clarify to the reader that I am in no way suggesting that I have heard the Lord perfectly, or word for word. I do feel, however, that I have received a message from Him, and I have tried my best to be true in communicating *the essence* of His message. On this issue, Rick Joyner has said, "Because prophecy is a gift of the Holy Spirit, we must treat everything that comes from Him as holy, but because it comes through humans, it must not be considered infallible." [1]

For those who are unsure or unfamiliar with prophecy, I recommend two resources by Rick Joyner, a man of integrity who is experienced and very well-respected in the field. For a comprehensive study, his book, *The Prophetic Ministry*, [2] in its entirety is highly instructive. For those who want a brief, but superb, overview of the field of prophecy, I recommend one of his latest books entitled *The Call*, especially the fifteen-page Introduction. [3] In addition, there are other fine prophetic voices the Lord is raising up in this hour, including Bishop Bill Hamon and Kim Clement, both of whom have excellent teaching material on the subject.

In the Bible, from Genesis to Revelation, we read of our loving heavenly Father communicating with His children. He not only walked with Adam and Eve in the cool of the day, He also talked with them. He spoke to Noah about the impending flood and gave him specific instructions for the construction of the ark. He spoke to Abraham repeatedly regarding His covenant with him. He spoke to King David about how his seed would sit on the throne. He spoke to Daniel through dreams and visions.

The Lord also spoke to Samuel, beginning when he was a very young child. Eli, the priest in charge of the young prophet, taught him to say, *"Speak, Lord, for your servant is listening"* (1 Samuel 3:9, NIV).

In this day, may we, too, cry out from our hearts, *"Speak, Lord, for your servant is listening."* For, as the people of God, we desperately need to hear His voice and to see from His perspective. Without a vision we perish, especially if we are without HIS vision.

My heart-prayer is that Jesus will do for us what He

did for His disciples immediately before His ascension: *"And He opened their understanding, that they might comprehend the Scriptures"* (Luke 24:45, NKJ). I further pray for each of us:

> *That the God of our Lord Jesus Christ, the Father of glory, may give to you the spirit of wisdom and revelation in the knowledge of Him, the eyes of your understanding being enlightened; that you may know what is the hope of His calling, what are the riches of the glory of His inheritance in the saints, and what is the exceeding greatness of His power toward us who believe, according to the working of His mighty power.*
> Ephesians 1:17-19, NKJ

Amen! I believe it is the Lord's purpose to reveal to the reader the reality and hope of this new day, thus bringing divine perspective in regard to the critical hour in which we live. How can we get to our destination if we do not first know where we are along the prophetic timetable? I will say many times and in many different ways in the following pages that we are not only in the last days, but more specifically, we have entered a window of time that could be referred to as the season of restoration, or the day of Elijah, which precedes the return of our Lord (see Malachi 4, Acts 3:19-21 and Matthew 17:11). This time period is different from all others that have gone before, and the better we understand it, the better we can cooperate with our God and prepare.

The world and our common enemy remind us daily of the dark and trying times in which we live. If we allow ourselves to focus on how things look around us, we will become discouraged and fearful, and, therefore, weak and ineffective. We must make the choice to seek out His prophetic voice and thereby receive the true perspective that brings life and encouragement.

We must allow the Lord to speak to us very deeply and personally, for He wants to transform us. The true Bride of Christ is now shedding the old graveclothes of slumber and carnality in order that she might receive her divine new apparel — her *Mantles of Glory*.

I trust that in the following pages each reader will see glimpses of his or her own future, of both the joys and the challenges that are sure to be a part of the coming days. The Holy Spirit is eager to reveal more specifically your own destiny and the mantle which you have been called to wear. It is time now to *find your place* in this great last-day battle drama and embrace your own unique mantle of anointing!

Endnotes:

1. Rich Joyner, *The Call*, Whitaker House (New Kensington, PA: 1999) p. 23).
2. Rick Joyner, *The Prophetic Ministry*, Morningstar Publications (Charlotte, NC: 1997).

Part I

A New Day Dawns

Chapter 1

The Spirit of Elijah Falls

A new day is dawning on the prophetic calendar, one which will prove to be unlike any other in history! This new day will bring a spiritual power that has never been seen on earth, indeed it will bring the power to do the *"greater works"* that Jesus prophesied for the last days (see John 14:12). This greater spiritual power will manifest itself in many diverse kinds of anointings that will fall as fiery *Mantles of Glory* upon the shoulders of God's faithful saints. These mantles will empower them to fulfill their destinies by accomplishing the Father's last-day purposes.

We are now entering the early-morning hours of this new day of fire prophesied by Malachi: *"For behold the day is coming, burning like a furnace ..."* (Malachi 4:1). The greater anointings are now arriving for the Body of Christ. The spiritual equipment and artillery required to fulfill the Father's purposes are beginning to be distributed to faithful servants and warriors throughout the world. The Body will begin to possess both the anointing and the financial provision necessary to be restored and to prepare the way for Christ's return.

The Greater Anointing

This greater anointing of power and provision will truly begin to destroy the yokes that have bound humanity for generations. It will also create divine appointments that will supernaturally prepare the 'net' of relationships for the tremendous end-time harvest of souls. As this enormous net is cast upon the whole earth at the Lord's bidding, multitudes will enter the latter-day 'ark' of God's salvation: *"But as the days of Noah were, so also will the coming of the Son of Man be"* (Matthew 24:37-39, NKJ).

Long ago, the prophet Elijah endured three and a half years of drought, only to awaken one morning to the joyful sound of destiny's alarm clock announcing God's appointed hour for rain. And now, many centuries later, we too are hearing destiny's alarm clock. The Elijahs of our day are being awakened and called by God to bring forth the spiritual rain. We are being called up the mountain of God in order to squat, travail and birth in the Spirit, to bring forth that which God has already promised through the word of His prophets.

Latter-Day Seers

The Lord is graciously applying the eye-salve of the

Holy Spirit to the eyes of the hungry in this hour, imparting the gift of revelation so that we can see into the mysteries of the end. The Scriptures say that the end will be *"as the days of Noah,"* and was Noah not *"divinely warned of things not yet seen"* (Hebrews 11:7, NKJ) so that he could prepare? Did not God Himself come to Noah speaking of the future and giving Noah very specific instructions regarding his role in it?

Even King Nebuchadnezzar, a heathen king, realized that the God of the prophet Daniel was *"a revealer of secrets"* (Daniel 2:47, KJV). Daniel was given much revelation into the secrets of his own times, and also of the end, but he was then instructed by God to *"seal up the book until the time of the end"* (Daniel 12:4, NKJ).

Could it be that we now have the great honor of receiving the same spirit of revelation, the mantle of anointing, that was upon Daniel in his day? Could it be that many of us will be anointed to see together, so that the mysteries and secrets of the end might be reopened and revealed so that we can prepare, fulfilling our destinies? I, for one, say, "Yes!"

Visions of God

I saw in the spirit realm a fiery comet coming into the earth's atmosphere. I understood that it was bringing with it greater spiritual power than had ever been seen. I further understood that it was the spirit of Elijah (see Matthew 17:11), the fiery anointing that would empower the Body of Christ to fulfill the Father's purposes of restoration. This greater power had been held and reserved in Heaven until just the right time, the time appointed by the Father, the time preceding the return of the Lord (see Malachi 4).

I observed an enormous, seemingly impenetrable, glass dome covering America. The glass vault was sealed around all geographic borders, and I realized that it symbolized the dark powers preventing the Church from receiving its victorious inheritance. Suddenly, a massive lightning bolt struck the dome, cracking the entire circumference, yet the dome remained intact.

Then water began to drip from the top of it. Coming from above, there was an intense pressure, and I knew it was only a matter of time before it would break, providing an 'open Heaven' over America. The icy, globe-like veil had power for a season. However, in God's prophetic timetable, He was sending His greater anointing, the spirit of Elijah, to destroy the yoke.

I was shown a large calendar fastened to a wall, and unexpectedly the hand of the Father started reaching toward it. His hand reached to pull up a new page, as one might change a wall calendar from month to month. He was just beginning to turn the calendar, and the latest month was not yet visible. However, by catching a glimpse from up under, I was able to discern that the new month was the season of Elijah, that prophetic time period before the return of the Lord in which all things would be restored (see Matthew 17:11).

In the first vision concerning the spirit of Elijah, the Lord took me back to Elizabeth of old, the wife of

The Spirit of Elijah Falls

Zacharias the priest. I saw that she, who had been barren for so long, conceived John the Baptist in her advanced age, so that the way might be prepared for Jesus. The Lord then took me to the last-day Church, and I observed that she, too, who also had been barren for so long, was now conceiving. The aged last-day Church was conceiving the spirit of Elijah, the spirit that would prepare the way for the Lord's return.

The Lord led me to Micah chapter four, which begins, *"It will come about in the last days..."* Micah prophesied about the daughter of Zion laboring in childbirth (Micah 4:9-10). The last-day Church is just now giving birth to the spirit of Elijah, to the anointing that will restore all things before Christ's return. The last-day Church is in travail. She is bringing forth that which will, in turn, bring forth the return of the King of Kings and the Lord of Lords.

The Spirit of Elijah Will Empower Mantles

The Lord is beginning to recruit a mighty company of men and women who will walk in fresh mantles of anointing and carry the greater spiritual power required to accomplish His latter-day purposes. When Elijah ascended to Heaven in the fiery whirlwind, it was his mantle that fell upon Elisha, signifying the transference of the anointing, which came in double measure. Likewise, in this day, many are receiving the mantles of Enoch, Abraham, Noah, Joshua and many others — also in double measure.

The firepower engine, or spiritual fuel, empowering these mantles is the spirit of Elijah which has been reserved in double portion for this appointed hour. Long ago, the prophet Malachi proclaimed, *"Behold, I will send you Elijah the prophet before the coming of the great and dreadful day of the Lord"* (Malachi 4:5, KJV). Much later, Jesus explained to His disciples, *"Elijah truly is coming first and will restore all things"* (Matthew 17:11, NKJ).

In the dawning of this fiery new day, we will begin to see men and women appearing out of obscurity as present-day Moseses, Daniels, Esthers and others. This awesome army will raise up standards of righteousness, confront powers of darkness, shift the course of nations, see fire fall from heaven and call for the spiritual rain to come forth. These warriors will see the enemy routed, Zion restored and the dead raised. As latter-day Noahs, we will watch as the vast harvest is gathered, and as latter-day John the Baptists, we will see the way prepared for the return of our Bridegroom.

This is truly that moment we have been waiting for. A new era is dawning, one unlike any other in history. Buckle your spiritual seat belts and hang on for the most glorious ride of your entire life: *"But to you who fear My name The Sun of Righteousness shall arise…"* (Malachi 4:2, NKJ). The day of restoration has begun.

Receive … Then, Run!

"Eat richly of My Word, and partake of My fiery presence, My beloved," says your Father. "You

The Spirit of Elijah Falls

must welcome it, honor it, nurture it, yield to it, and become it. You must allow it to grow inside you, consume you, and overtake you with holy passion and zeal for My latter-day purposes.

"Then run in the power of it to deliver not only your own country, but all the nations. Run with the fiery feet that Malachi prophesied. Gird up your loins and run with the legs of Elijah to overtake the chariots of Ahab. Then, mount up with the wings of eagles, with your new mantle of double anointing and glory, and fly into your destiny, accomplishing all that I have foreordained for you. *For I am with you to do it!*" promises your Father.

Who will take the torch of His hope and run into the highways and byways of lost humanity, revealing the glory of the Lord to the ends of the earth?

Chapter 2

The Curtain Is Going Up On the Final Battle

The curtain is just now going up on the greatest 'battle-drama' of all the ages. The Father-Director is searching and auditioning for those dreaded warrior-actors and actresses who are willing to pay the ultimate price, who will forsake all because of their love and passion for Him and His latter-day purposes:

> *For the eyes of the* LORD *move to and fro throughout the earth that He may strongly support those whose heart is completely His.* 2 Chronicles 16:9

God is calling for those who will rise up in the great last-day anointing and take up their own personal mantles of destiny. He is looking for those who will run into the highways and the byways of lost humanity, showing forth His glory even to the ends of the earth. He is searching for those valiant ones whose Holy Ghost performance will reveal the love, victory and kingship of Jesus, winning the nations.

The backdrop of this great last-day drama is the 'deep darkness' that is upon the face of the earth today (see Isaiah 60:2). Violent streets are filled with desperate, hopeless youth crying out for a reason to live. Many homes and families resemble empty and bloody battlefields, while seniors have been thrown away and forgotten. The norm of the day is lust, deceit, perversion and greed. Even much of the Church has been sick, impotent and bound by powers of religious tradition and witchcraft — hardly a place of refuge or healing. Nations are torn apart by ethnic and racial wars, and worldwide there are earthquakes, plagues and famines, as prophesied for the end.

> "We need some Good News," cries the Father-Director. "Who will carry My hope to the hopeless in this darkest hour? Who will run with the torch of My fire and bear witness of *'the true light which coming into the world, enlightens every man'*?" [1]

Where Are the Dreaded Latter-Day Warriors?

The divine stage is now set, the world is crying out, and the whole of creation is groaning for the revelation of the true sons of the living God. Where are the players, the great latter-day warriors, who will rise up in this new

The Curtain Is Going Up on the Final Battle

anointing and take the glory of the Lord to a dying world? Who will tell men, in the power of the Spirit, that a Savior has been born, a Deliverer has come? Who will tell them of the great love and forgiveness of the Father, and who will tell them of a bloody cross called Calvary? Who will tell them that their debt has been paid in full and that the veil between them and the Father was torn two thousand years ago? Who will tell them that Jesus is the Way back, and in this day of deceit, who will tell them the truth, that He is the only Door to the Father? As the Lord asked Isaiah the prophet, *"Whom shall I send, and who will go for Us?"* (Isaiah 6:8).

Where are those last-day warriors, of whom the devil and his hosts are terrified because they hold to their testimony of Jesus, the dreaded Champion of those who believe? And where are those who will not love their lives even unto the very death? Where are those who are not only willing to die for Christ, but also to live for Him, dying daily? Where are those warriors who know their God and who will do great exploits in His name?

Where are those warriors who have been stoned and left for dead on the dung heaps of religion, betrayal and witchcraft, only to be raised up by that same precious Holy Spirit that raised Jesus from the dead? Where are those warriors who will pay the ultimate price, passing through that very narrow place called Golgotha, that they might say as Jesus, *"for the ruler of this world is coming, and he has nothing in Me"* (John 14:30, NKJ)?

Are you among the warriors who have given the Lord your last bit of flour and oil during the long years of drought and famine, as the widow of Zarephath, only to receive back His provision and double resurrection power? Are you among the noble, mighty men and women whose hearts burn for nothing but their King's desire, just as David's mighty men who broke through the camp of the Philistine army to give their king what he longed for, a drink from the well of Bethlehem (see 2 Samuel 23:15-16)?

And are you among the warriors whom the devil thought he had finished off, that are scarred and walking with a limp, but who live and breathe to do nothing but destroy the works of darkness through His fiery anointing, honoring the Lamb wherever He goes in this late hour? Are you among the warriors who consider all in their lives as nothing, except for Jesus, and Him crucified and resurrected?

> "I am looking," says the Father, "for the warriors who have the eyes of eagles, seeing into the future the unfolding battle of the ages. I am looking for those warriors who see the glorious bride being adorned as the heavenly Jerusalem. [2] And finally," says the Father, "I am looking for the warriors who see the great harvest coming forth into the massive eternal ark, culminating in the victory and return of the Lamb."

Warriors Are Discarding Their Graveclothes

"Where," asks the Father-Director, "are the warriors who will now throw off the slumbering

The Curtain Is Going Up on the Final Battle

graveclothes of the long wilderness-night, looking to the Holy Ghost Wardrober for the divine apparel for this bright new morning? It is time now for each warrior to receive his unique anointing, the *Mantles of Glory* and grace that fit just right, for the fulfillment of his or her own destiny!

"Wake up, My latter-day warriors, and take up your glorious mantles of destiny!" challenges your Father-Commander. "I have prepared them for you from long ago for the accomplishment of My latter-day purposes."

The graveclothes of yesteryear are now being discarded, giving way to glorious new mantles of end-time destiny, even as beautiful butterflies emerging out of their old cocoons. This greater anointing of the spirit of Elijah will begin to manifest in many diverse and creative mantles, each one representing unique giftings fashioned by the Holy Ghost Wardrober.

Each mantle has been designed and tailored according to its wearer's callings and elections that were foreordained by the Father. The very character and nature of Jesus Himself constitutes the structure and fiber of each mantle. Each mantle is empowered by the greater anointing of the Holy Spirit that has been reserved for this hour. Each mantle carries the power that is needed to fulfill the unique destiny of its wearer.

Mantles to Accomplish the Father's Purpose

These mantles of anointing shimmer with the brilliant heavenly rainbow colors of the glory of the Lord that is now arising upon the Bride of Christ (see Isaiah 60:1-3). These mantles will pick up the wind of His Spirit and cause her to fly high as the eagles. These mantles of destiny will begin to accomplish the greater works Jesus prophesied (see John 14:12), as they have been prepared and reserved in double portion for this day of 'deep darkness' that is upon the face of the earth. These *Mantles of Glory* represent crucifixion of the flesh and the emergence of the life of the Spirit, manifesting in the true rulership and headship of Jesus as Lord over His Body. Glory to the Lamb!

> "Through these mantles of glory," explains the Lord, "I will destroy the works of the evil one, and I will prepare, restore and glorify My Bride. I will send the mantle of Noah upon many who will then draw multitudes upon multitudes of the lost and dying into the ark of My salvation. I will send the mantle of Nehemiah upon many in order to rebuild the walls of My beloved Jerusalem. I will mantle the Bride with the heart of Rebekah, so that she will respond quickly to the Holy Spirit, saying *'I will go'* as she departs on her journey to meet her beloved Bridegroom."

Quickly, Find Your Places!

Curtains up, warriors! Places, places, dreaded latter-day warriors. The Director-Commander is on the set and ready, for the appointed time has come. The greatest harvest/audience of all the ages is very ripe and is hanging in the balance. The Lamb-Bridegroom is waiting for His Bride to prepare the way for His return, while the great cloud of witnesses are watching and cheering. Quickly, look to Him to find your mantles, your places, latter-day warriors!

Endnotes:

1. John 1:9.
2. See Revelation 21:9-10.

Chapter 3

Receive Your Virility, Abraham

As the people of God in these critical last days, we must prepare by putting on the faith mantle of our Father Abraham, who, after enduring many years of waiting, 'looked up' and welcomed the visitation of the Lord and the fulfillment of his destiny!

> *Now the Lord appeared to him [Abraham] by the oaks of Mamre, while he was sitting at the tent door in the heat of the day. And when he lifted up his eyes and looked, behold, three men were standing opposite him; and when he saw them, he ran from the tent door to meet them, and bowed himself to the earth, and said, "My lord, if now I have found favor in your sight, please do not pass your servant by."* Genesis 18:1-3

Father Abraham's response to the arrival of the three heavenly messengers is a model for us, demonstrating how we must respond in this day to God's visitation of revival and restoration. We also must 'look up' in faith and run to welcome His outpouring and the fulfillment of our end-time destinies. We, too, as the people of God, have waited a very long time for the fulfillment of our promises, indeed, for this new season of empowering. It is now coming upon us, but we must be diligent to look up, welcome it and run with it. Let us not be passed by.

"Wake Up, My Warriors!"

God is setting His heavenly alarm clocks in the early morning hours of this new day, waking up His last-day warrior-fathers and mothers!

> "Wake up, My warriors, My latter-day Abrahams and Sarahs," says the Lord, "and look up, for your redemption is drawing nigh. You are truly living in the generation that many longed to see. Time will not stand still for you, for this is the appointed time in which I will favor you. [1]

> "This is truly the hour of deliverance and restoration for My people, and this is the hour of My vengeance toward the evil one. The great harvest will not wait, for the time is short. Wake up, My latter-day fathers and mothers, look up to your faithful Father, and then run to welcome My greater anointings and purposes that I am

directing in this strategic hour. Learn from your Father Abraham; believe and receive Me. It is time to lay hold of your destinies, My children," exhorts your loving Father.

Through Faith and Patience

When Abraham was ninety-nine years old and sitting by the trees of Mamre (see Genesis 18:1), surely he must have recalled how Yahweh had commanded him decades earlier to leave his father's house and go to a land that he knew not of. He must have cherished the time Yahweh had come to him, putting him to sleep and making a blood covenant with him, promising him great things. And he must have pondered his disappointment in Ishmael, the child of his flesh, the child whom divine destiny had somehow eluded.

How could he forget the time Yahweh had changed his name from Abram to Abraham, calling him *'the father of many nations,'* while challenging him to circumcise all those in his household as a sign of the covenant? He remembered the promises, he pondered, and he waited. He endured by seeing Him who is unseen, and yes, he and Sarah believed Yahweh was able. Theirs was a promise that was difficult to fathom. The number of their descendants would be *"as the stars of the heavens,"* Yahweh had said, *"and of the dust of the earth."*

Abraham sat in the heat of the day at his tent door, anticipating and watching. Perhaps Yahweh will choose this day to visit again. This was the same Abraham who believed God, and it was reckoned to him as righteousness, and this was the Abraham that had been abundantly blessed with many flocks, herds, possessions and servants. This was the Abraham, still waiting for His promise, waiting for the fulfillment of that divine seed of faith and destiny that had been implanted into the womb of his and Sarah's hearts so many years before.

Heavenly Messengers Arrive

That glorious day of destiny finally arrived for Abraham, starting just like any other day, as he was found sitting by his tent door in the heat of the day.

> "Even so," says the Lord, "many of My people today also think this is just another day, but they must understand that I am coming to them in this day, after so many years of waiting. I am coming to them in the heat of this fiery new day, the day that Malachi saw would *'burn like an oven.'* [2] My last-day fathers and mothers, I am visiting you today, empowering you to conceive and birth your last-day destinies," promises your faithful Father.

So Abraham's moment of destiny finally arrived. When the three messengers of Good News came, was the father of our faith found asleep? Or had he become dull and feeble from all the years of waiting? Perhaps

Receive Your Virility, Abraham

he was bitter with doubt and accusation toward Yahweh for the decades of emptiness and delay? Or was he so busy caring for his many possessions and his wealth that he had become self-focused and distracted, missing the heavenly visitors?

No, the father of the faith did not miss his moment of opportunity, but ran toward it with all his might.

In Hope Against Hope

Abraham looked up, seeing the heavenly messengers walking toward him. He lifted up the eyes of his heart, believing that Yahweh was still able these many years later. Even after all the years of weariness and heart-sickness from hope that was long deferred, he chose, by faith, to look up to behold the messengers of destiny. He was looking up into the heavens of God's faithfulness, expecting and watching, because he knew that the city whose builder and maker is God, was a heavenly city:

> *In hope against hope he believed, in order that he might become a father of many nations.... And without becoming weak in faith he contemplated his own body, now as good as dead since he was about a hundred years old, and the deadness of Sarah's womb; yet with respect to the promise of God, he did not waver in unbelief, but grew strong in faith, giving glory to God, and being fully assured that what He had promised, He was able also to perform.*
>
> Romans 4:18-21

Look Up

"This is the critical hour in which My people must again look up," says the Father. "Yes, it is true that this is the hour I have chosen to begin to pour out My Spirit upon all flesh, but you must position yourself by looking up in faith to receive all that I am doing."

It is time to rouse yourself from your long wilderness-slumber and shake off the graveclothes of dullness, arising to welcome the glory of your destinies, last-day Abrahams and Sarahs. It is time to put aside business as usual and focus on the Lord and His business. It is time to *"seek those things which are above, where Christ is, sitting at the right hand of God,"* to *"set your mind on things above, not on things on the earth"* (Colossians 3:1-2, NKJ).

"As you look up in this hour, My people," asks the Lord, "can you not discern My form on the spiritual horizon? Are you not catching glimpses of the Sun of Righteousness as He is arising to those who fear His name? [3] As you quiet yourself and seek Me, are you not finding My presence nearer and stronger than ever before? Surely you are hearing more and more of My messenger-voices prophesying last-day revival and restoration. From sea to shining sea, My true prophets are prophesying that the day of the fulfillment of your destiny is at hand," says the Father.

Father Abraham Runs

As Father Abraham looked up long ago and saw the three messengers coming, he immediately recognized that they were from God. He wasted no time in making theological determinations. He called no board meetings to gather data and vote, nor did he consult with the religious and denominational heads of state. But he did what was in his heart to do. After so many years of waiting, enduring and believing, he could not help himself. He R-A-N to His Lord: *'and when he saw them, he ran from the tent door to meet them.'* Abraham was compelled of the Spirit of God, for this was the moment he had been waiting for!

> "And may you, too, My last-day fathers and mothers, cast off all constraints, and run with all your might to welcome Me and My end-time purposes," exhorts your Father. "May you receive the grace of Father Abraham in abandoning yourselves wholeheartedly to Me. May you be delivered from the religious and man-pleasing spirits that would seek to discredit this move, this greater anointing that I have reserved for this hour. And may you be delivered from reliance upon reasoning, being set free in your hearts and

spirits to worship and serve Me, the one true living God. May you dance with all your might, as David, as you welcome home the precious ark of My abiding presence and purpose in this late hour."

Please, Do Not Pass Your Servant By!

After running to the messengers, Abraham bowed low to honor and worship Yahweh, as He had come bringing Good News. He said, *"My Lord, if I have now found favor in Your sight, do not pass on by Your servant"* (Genesis 18:3, NKJ). The father of the faith humbly, but boldly, seized his opportunity to ask for favor, to not be passed by. In this most critical time in history, let us also seek God's favor, beseeching Him to not pass us by in this hour of destiny. Please, O precious Father, do not pass us by in this hour of empowering and impartation.

Abraham and Sarah immediately began to serve these heavenly messengers, bringing water for the washing of their feet and preparing food. As they stood together under the tree eating, Yahweh announced that it was time for Sarah to conceive the child of promise. It was time for the covenant to be fulfilled. That one word, that one encounter with the living God changed Abraham's life forever. When Jehovah spoke this prophetic word to him, Abraham became virile. In that very moment, he received the anointing to become father to many nations.

Receive Your Virility, Abraham

The voice of God is awesome! It is the voice that imparts virility and begets destiny:

The voice of the Lord is over the waters…
The voice of the Lord is powerful;
The voice of the Lord is full of majesty.
The voice of the Lord breaks the cedars…
The voice of the Lord divides the flames of fire.
The voice of the Lord shakes the wilderness…
The voice of the Lord makes the deer give birth,
And strips the forests bare;
And in His temple everyone says, 'Glory!'
                                    Psalm 29:3-9, NKJ

In this strategic day, we too must be listening for and welcoming that heavenly voice that creates life, that voice that changes everything in a single moment. We must seek it, honor it and heed it.

"I Am Casting Out the Bondwoman and Her Son"

When Sarah overheard the messengers' announcement, she laughed, as she was ninety years of age and well beyond the age of childbearing. But Yahweh replied, *"Is anything too hard for the Lord?"*

"Yes," says the Lord, "I again hear the laughter of many Sarahs in this day, so I ask, My people, 'Is anything too hard for Me?' Did I not purposely delay, so that Sarah would know that the life I placed in her womb was of My Spirit rather than of her flesh? For I am He who flung the stars and galaxies into existence by the mere word and breath of My mouth. And I am He who created the oceans that roar and the sea creatures that they contain.

"Am I not able to fulfill that which I have spoken?" asks the Omnipotent One. "Has My arm been shortened since Abraham's day?

"In My prophetic timetable, I have chosen this very hour to launch you into the fulfillment of your destinies, My last-day Abrahams and Sarahs. I have purposely delayed, allowing your Ishmaels and fleshly efforts to wane and grow weary in the dry wildernesses of waiting. Know that, in this hour, I am casting out the bondwoman and her son, Ishmael, the flesh, for he cannot be heir with My son, Isaac, the child of latter-day promise," declares the Lord. [4]

"I Am the God of Today"

In the past, we have known our Lord as the God of the promises, but in this day, we will come to know Him as the God *of the fulfillment of the promises.* Even as Abraham knew Him for many years as the God of the "I will," he came to know Him as the God of the "I am doing." He came to know Him as the God of

Receive Your Virility, Abraham

virility, of conception and of Sarah's big belly. He came to know Him as the God of his son Isaac, as the God of his grandson Jacob and as the God of his great-grandson Joseph.

And from the corridors of Heaven, Abraham came to know the Lord as the God of Moses and Joshua and as the God of the children of Israel, who were as vast as the stars of heaven, and as vast as the sands on the seashore, in fulfillment of the covenant. Father Abraham came to know God as the One who fulfilled His word, empowering Abraham to truly become the father of many nations.

> "You, too, in this day," says the Lord, "will come to know Me as the God who fulfills His promises. You will know Me as the God of Elijah and Elisha who restores double to *your* families. You will come to know Me as the God of Daniel, who gives *you* wisdom and revelation for the kings and leaders of *your* day. You will know Me as the God of Moses, who parts *your* Red Seas and drowns *your* Egyptian enemies in the outpouring of My last-day anointing. You will know Me as the God of Noah, as I work through *you* to build the greatest ark of all the ages.

> "You will know Me in this hour as the God of Nehemiah," says the Lord, "as I rebuild the walls of My beloved Jerusalem. You will know Me as the God of Rebekah, as I prepare My Bride for

her waiting Bridegroom, adorning her with the lavish double-portion gifts of glory. You will know Me as the God who answers and delivers by fire, and as the God who rules His Church, executing vengeance on His enemies. [5] You will indeed come to know Me as the God of Abraham who imparts the anointing of spiritual virility, sending forth the mantle of fatherhood and motherhood on many in this late hour!"

The Mantle of Fatherhood

"If you will believe Me now as My servant Abraham did," says your Father, "I will impart to you spiritual virility, that you may have the anointing necessary for the fathering and the fulfillment of your destiny. As the Father-of-All, I am now imparting the spirit and mantle of fatherhood and motherhood to those who, through proven faith and patience, are prepared to birth and father their Isaacs, their last-day destinies."

As the people of God, we must not miss this greatest moment in history, this new day of restoration that is set before us. We must embrace the fulfillment of our callings, taking up the heavenly batons and running with endurance this last great marathon before us. How very sad it would be to look back from eternity only to realize that we had missed our chance in participating in the greatest battle drama, the greatest harvest, the world had ever known! We must *not* miss that chance.

"I Am Imparting Virility"

"My last-day fathers and mothers, this is the hour of My impartation," says the Lord. "I am now imparting prophetic gifts and mantles of double-portion anointing for the accomplishment of My purposes. Indeed, just as I came to Abraham after so many years of waiting, so am I coming to you today. You must continue to look up, to watch and wait for Me. Through even one encounter with Me, even one visitation, I am able to impart to you spiritual virility, even as I did to Abraham.

"After decades and even centuries of My Church's impotence and barrenness, I am now imparting to her the spiritual virility and anointing that is needed to father and mother all My end-time purposes," announces the Lord. "Indeed, know that I, as the Lord of the heavens and the earth, the Lord of the times and the seasons, have chosen this prophetic hour in which to show forth My glory into all the earth. I have ordained that My glory will shine through you, My people, as you arise and receive your fresh, new mantles of double-portion anointings! [6]

"Do not be distracted, nor sit idly by in passivity and indecision, My beloved children! For it is imperative that you R-U-N to welcome My last-day visitation and purposes. You must honor them, laying hold of them with all your might. Learn from your Father Abraham, and do not be passed by in this most critical hour of destiny," exhorts your concerned Father.

Your old men shall dream dreams,
Your young men shall see visions.
And also on My menservants and on My maidservants
I will pour out My Spirit in those days.

Joel 2:28-29, NKJ

Amen!

Endnotes:

1. See Psalm 102:13.
2. Malachi 4:1.
3. Malachi 4:2.
4. See Galatians 4:30.
5. See Isaiah 61:2.
6. See Isaiah 60:1.

The true bride will be found in only one place in this late hour. She will be found at the well, drawing living waters for the nations and the peoples of the earth.

Chapter 4

The True Bride Found at the Well

As Father Abraham was advancing in years, his thoughts began to turn toward his son and heir, as Isaac was already forty years old and did not yet have a wife. Father Abraham called forth his oldest, most respected servant and sent him to seek a bride for his son, commanding him to go to his homeland, to his own country and relatives to find her. Abraham promised his servant that the angel of the Lord would go before him to assist him on his mission.

Father Abraham Seeks a Bride for His Son Isaac

Abraham's servant then traveled to his master's homeland, to Mesopotamia, to the city of Nahor, in search of Isaac's bride. He must have thought to himself, "Where should I look for the bride? Perhaps she will be found in the marketplace shopping for her family, or perhaps she will be found among the other young women, playfully frolicking in the street." But because the servant had traveled a long distance and was thirsty, he stopped first at the well outside the city where some women were drawing water.

Inquiring of the Lord by presenting a fleece, he asked, "Lord, as I ask for a drink, let it be the woman who says, 'Drink and I will water your camels also.' " Before he was even able to finish his prayer, Rebekah, the daughter of Bethuel, of the relatives of Abraham, came down to the spring to fill her jar. The servant ran to her and this conversation resulted:

The servant ... said, "Please let me drink a little water from your jar."
And she said, "Drink, my lord"; and she quickly lowered her jar to her hand, and gave him a drink.
Now when she had finished giving him a drink, she said, "I will draw also for your camels until they have finished drinking."
So she quickly emptied her jar into the trough, and ran back to the well to draw, and she drew for all [ten of] his camels. Genesis 24:17-18

Father God Seeks a Bride for His Son Jesus

"Even so, as Father God," says the Lord, "in the fullness of time, are My thoughts now turning toward My Son and Heir, Jesus, and His need of a wife; for He has waited a very long time indeed. I am now calling forth My most trusted Servant, My precious Holy Spirit, to seek a Bride for the Bridegroom. I am today sending forth the very hosts of heaven to seek and to gather, from the four corners of the earth, My Son's Bride, that she might be prepared and adorned for the soon return of her Bridegroom," says the Father.

As Abraham's servant was drawn to the well in his search for Isaac's bride, even so is the Servant-Spirit also being drawn to the well in this day, to the well of living water, in search of the Bride. She will be found in only one place; she will be found at the true Well of salvation through the blood of Jesus Christ. The latter-day Bride will be drawing from the Well of the Good News of the Gospel.

The Bride Draws From One True Source

The Bride will draw only from the true Well whose healing waters make the lame to walk and the blind to see. She will draw from that wondrous Well whose merciful waters heal the brokenhearted and comfort those who mourn. She will draw from the delivering waters that set at liberty those who are bound and open the door for the prisoners. She will be found drawing from that glorious Well that brings *"beauty for ashes, the oil of joy for mourning,"* and *"the garment of praise for the spirit of heaviness"* (Isaiah 61:3, NKJ). She will draw deeply in these latter days from the Well who confirms His Word with mighty signs and wonders following.

The Bride will draw living water only from the Well that is fed by that river of scarlet that ever flows from Calvary, from Christ's sacrifice and death on the cross. She will be found drawing deeply of waters of repentance, of the forgiveness of sins and of new life. She will begin to show forth the character of the Lamb of God, as she draws from the rivers of love, joy and peace, and from the deep waters of patience, kindness and goodness. As she draws from Heaven's pure waters, she will begin to show forth faithfulness, gentleness and self-control (see Galatians 5:22).

"I Am Calling the Bride Out"

"I am drawing the Bride to the true Well of My living water in this day," explains the Father. "I am calling her out from among those who are drawing from the dead, stale waters of carnality and religion. I am also delivering her from the tainted and polluted waters of deception. She will not be found drawing from among strange and humanistic mixtures of water:

" *'Does a fountain send out from the same opening both fresh and bitter water? Can a fig tree, my brethren, produce olives, or a vine produce figs? Neither can salt water produce fresh.'*   James 3:11-12

> "I have also warned, *'A little leaven leavens the whole lump.'* [1] My glorious latter-day Bride will be found drawing only from the purity and simplicity of devotion to Jesus, her Bridegroom."

We must not be deceived into thinking there are different wells and different streams leading to eternal life. We have been forewarned in His Word that there would be much deception in the last days. Did Jesus not tell us plainly that He alone is the Door of the sheep, that His Father is the Doorkeeper and that anyone who tries to come in any other way is a thief and a robber (see John 10:8)?

> *If anyone enters through Me, he shall be saved, and shall go in and out, and find pasture. The thief comes only to steal, and kill, and destroy; I came that they might have life, and might have it abundantly. I am the good shepherd; the good shepherd lays down His life for the sheep.* John 10:9-11

Be warned, dear ones, that New Age humanism, self-help psychology and introversion have infiltrated the Church. Secular, carnal theories of counseling, mind-control, motivation and self-improvement have been brought into the Church, wrapped up in Christian paper and then preached from our pulpits. Was the work of Calvary deficient, that our pulpits must now call upon psychiatrists, counselors and other spiritual gurus? Do the experts and Ph.D.'s understand the cares of the human heart better than the One who created them?

> "Have My blood, My Word and My Holy Spirit lost their power to raise the dead, comfort those who mourn and restore the brokenhearted?" asks the all-powerful Father. "Is anything too difficult for Me?"

"Keep the Blood Central!"

> "Beware, My people! Remember the work of Calvary by keeping the cleansing and life-giving power of My blood central in your lives. Give your needs, your wounds and your problems over to Me and to My Spirit of life and healing! Behold Me in My Word and glory so that you will be transformed by the power of it:

But we all, with unveiled face, beholding as in a mirror the glory of the Lord, are being transformed into the same image from glory to glory, just as from the Lord, the Spirit.   2 Corinthians 3:18

In this day of narcissim, we must be delivered from the snare of digging into the dead bones of our past and from the confusion of reasoning and introversion. We must be delivered from needing our ears tickled, and we must beware of the sophisticated intrigue of humanism. We must, instead, focus on Him and His

The True Bride Found at the Well

life-giving thoughts. We must worship the King of Glory and be transformed by the fire of His presence.

Let us come forth into the bright clear light of our resurrected Savior. We must focus on Jesus, His work of the cross and His last-day plan. Did He not make the truth and mysteries of the Gospel simple enough for babes?

> *Jesus answered and said, "I thank You, Father, Lord of heaven and earth, that You have hidden these things from the wise and prudent and have revealed them to babes. Even so, Father, for so it seemed good in Your sight."* Matthew 11:25-26, NKJ

A River of Life

Beloved Bride, is not the Lord's river the only river of life? Did He not reveal to the prophet Ezekiel the river of life flowing from the sanctuary (see Ezekiel 47)? It started as a trickle, but it grew into a mighty river that could not be forded. Wherever the river went, things would live *"so everything will live where the river goes"* (Ezekiel 47:9).

The same river of life was revealed to another prophet named Isaiah: *"Ho! Everyone who thirsts, come to the waters…"* (Isaiah 55:1, NKJ). The river was shown many years later to the apostle John on the Island of Patmos: *"And he showed me a pure river of water of life, clear as crystal, proceeding from the throne of God and of the Lamb"* (Revelation 22:1, NKJ).

Jesus revealed Himself to the Samaritan woman as that same river of living water, as He sat on Jacob's well that day long ago, waiting for her to come (see John 4). He explained to her:

Everyone who drinks of this water [in Jacob's well], shall thirst again; but whoever drinks of the water that I shall give him shall never thirst; but the water that I shall give him shall become in him a well of water springing up to eternal life. John 4:13-14

As the woman responded and asked Jesus for this living water, He began to speak with her intimately about her life, her past and even the future. He began to speak to her about true worship, and He revealed Himself to her personally as her Messiah.

"As you encounter Me in this hour as the Living Water," says the Lord, "I will converse with you intimately, not only about your past and present, but I will speak to you especially of the deep and glorious waters of your future, as I did to this woman. For My river of life knows no boundaries of yesterdays and todays. Yes, My clean river of mercy washes away the sins, regrets and wounds of the past, and the fresh, pure current brings grace and strength for today. But My river is also the river of the future which pulls you into your destiny. This life-giving river is drawing you into the fulfillment of your callings

The True Bride Found at the Well

and revealing to you the great and mighty things I will do. For I will work both in you and through you, in these critical last days," rejoices the Lord of your future.

"I Am Waiting for You at the Well"

"This is the prophetic hour, My Bride, when you will encounter Me as your Living Water. As you go about your daily business as the Samaritan woman who came to draw water at Jacob's well that day long ago, you will encounter Me as she did, waiting for you at the well."

The faithful Father is beginning to satisfy and fill the deep thirst and longing we have carried within our souls for so very long. He is bringing the freshness and coolness of His living water to our parched and empty places, for this is the hour of our restoration:

For waters shall burst forth in the wilderness, and streams in the desert. The parched ground shall become a pool, and the thirsty land springs of water.
Isaiah 35:6-7, NKJ

We, as the Bride, must come and let the Lord's healing, refreshing waters begin to overflow us and wash away our weariness. Is this not indeed the river that He chose to cleanse, restore and prepare us for our Bridegroom? We must allow the fresh waters of life from His throne to envelope and transform us from one realm of glory to another. This latter-day river of fire and holiness will wash away the dullness, earthiness and lusts of the world. As the Bride, we must not only drink from this glorious river; we must immerse ourselves completely in it, so that all stains, spots and wrinkles will be washed away. *"To her it was granted to be arrayed in fine linen, clean and bright"* (Revelation 19:8, NKJ).

"Come Out Into the Deep Where My Glory Dwells"

"You must yield to My river yet more and more, My Bride," exhorts the Father, "and allow it to pick you up and to carry you into your destiny. Do not be fearful of the increasing strength and current of My river, but trust it to buoy you up above the rocks, tree stumps and obstacles in what has been the dry riverbed of your life. Let this mighty river lift you now above the obstacles that have prevented and impeded your progress for years, even for decades. Is this not the hour of My sovereign rule in the earth?" asks the Lord of all. "Indeed, this river of life is growing both deeper and stronger, and you will feel it drawing and pulling you yet more and more into the heart of My latter-day purposes in the earth."

The prophet Ezekiel observed the river as it grew from a trickle to ankle-deep. He then saw the river rise to his knees, and even to his waist. The river be-

The True Bride Found at the Well

came so deep that Ezekiel could not cross it (see Ezekiel 47:1-5).

As we yield to the Lord's river more and more, we will truly begin to 'lose' our lives that we might finally find them in Him. As we let go of our own self-life, we will begin to be overtaken by the life-flow of the river, the life-flow which originates from Him and from His throne (see Revelation 22:1).

We must cease holding on to the banks of the river, and we must cease staying in the shallow waters if we want to be buoyed up and carried into the heart of God's purposes in this hour. Will we continue to trust in our own fleshly efforts to support ourselves, or will we let go completely, trusting in the faithfulness of His river to sustain and buoy us up? We must let go of our past and our own plans for our future and trust Him as He draws us out into the deep.

> "My dearest Bride, come out into the deep where My glory dwells," beckons the King of Glory. "Come out into the deep where you will behold Me in My latter-day glory and be transformed. Let Me draw you away from your past and all that has held you captive. Come, receive of the life of My river. Come out into the deep where I am waiting for you," calls the Lord again.

Transformed by the River

The life-changing currents are not along the banks,

dear Bride, but rather in the heart of the river. As we offer ourselves to the Lord and yield to Him, He will draw us out and swirl around us with His deep, pure, transforming waters of life. We must cease trying to change ourselves, for it is futile. Jesus alone knows our highest callings and elections, and He alone can transform us into all that He has called us to be in these strategic last days.

Yes, it is true that the Father's deep currents are strong, unfamiliar and perhaps even frightening at times, but know that it is love unfathomable that is at work in these mysterious and merciful waters. None of His dealings are in vain, dear ones — only for our eternal good. Even the sinless Son had to yield Himself to the deep waters of Calvary in order for the Father's purposes to be accomplished. As we continue to focus on Him, rather than on our temporal circumstances, our momentary "light affliction" will work for us "a far more exceeding and eternal weight of glory" (2 Corinthians 4:17, NKJ).

Our Merciful Father Turns Up the Heat

Indeed, is this not the critical hour of thirst in the earth? In the heat of this new day, the day that the prophet Malachi saw that is *"burning like an oven"* (Malachi 4:1), there are multitudes upon multitudes who are in the valley of decision and are dying of thirst.

"I am turning up the heat in this hour,' says the

The True Bride Found at the Well

Lord, 'because of My mercy. Did I not say that those who hunger and thirst for righteousness are blessed, because I will fill them? [2]

"It is My lovingkindness and mercy that have brought forth the heat and thirst that will cause many to seek Me and My living water in this late hour and be delivered," explains the Lord. "The heat of this day is causing multitudes to cry out:

" *'As the deer pants for the water brooks,*
So pants my soul for You, O God.
My soul thirsts for God, for the living God.' "
Psalm 42:1-2, KJV

When Christ suffered all things on the cross on our behalf, He also suffered thirst. Did He not cry out, *"I am thirsty,"* just before His death (John 19:28)? The Living Water Himself hung upon the cross, suffering the thirst of the whole world. And did He not *"pour [Himself] out as a drink offering upon the sacrifice and service of your faith"* (Philippians 2:17)?

"Out of the depths of My love for all the peoples of the nations, I chose to leave glorious fellowship with My Father in Heaven, where I:

" *'...existed in the form of God, [but] did not regard equality with God a thing to be grasped, but emptied [Myself], taking the form of a bond-servant.... And being found in appearance as a man, [I] humbled [Myself] by becoming obedient to the point of death, even death on a cross."* Philippians 2:6-8

"As the Living Water, I poured Myself completely out for My beloved Bride, as well as for all the peoples, tongues, tribes and nations of the earth."

A River-Bed Bride

"This is your hour to be raised up and glorified, My Bride," says your Father:

*" 'Arise, shine, for your light has come,
And the glory of the Lord is risen upon you.'*
Isaiah 60:1

"I suffered the thirst of the whole world on the cross, so that you, in this strategic hour of restoration and harvest, might bring My glorious rivers of living water to those who are dying of thirst. I emptied Myself out that you, My beloved Bride, might be full and overflowing. I suffered the shame of the cross that you would reflect My honor and show forth My glory in these latter days. [3] A great exchange took place on the cross, where I took the sin and reproach of all men, that you might bear My honor and glory.

It is time to shine, My Bride, for your time has finally come!" rejoices the Bridegroom.

Beloved Bride, has not your belly become a wondrous 'river bed' in this hour, providing a vast channel through which the Lord can pour out His last-day blessings? And do not your willingness, your daily 'living sacrifices,' provide a suitable bed through which He may send His flood of heavenly bounties and riches?

The deep and glorious currents of His river have been continually eroding the sands of your own self-lives, providing an ever-larger and broader avenue for His resurrection life. As the obedient, surrendered Bride, you have offered to Him all the sands and cares of your lives, inviting the current of His river to twist and turn and shape the banks and boundaries of your lives according to His latter-day purposes.

It's Time to Stretch

Are you not indeed making a way for the return of the King of Glory? Even as Mary offered herself and her womb for the infant Jesus to make His first arrival into humanity, so has the beloved Bride also received His latter-day infant-purposes into her spiritual womb. In fact, she is now in labor, with birth pangs and contractions of the end that have suddenly come upon her. Dear Bride, you must understand that your riverbed belly is the very heavenly birth canal that is making a way for the Lord's return.

Yes, you are being stretched, beloved, and stretched and stretched some more. You sometimes feel that you will be stretched so much that you will be split apart, but know that it is not so, dear ones. The Father has formed you and called you for this critical hour and purpose, so know that He is standing with you in these last stages of your delivery.

> "It is time to yield and rest in Me," exhorts your Father, "knowing that I am taking over with the power and anointings of My birth pangs and contractions. Do not struggle and push in your own strength, for you will become weary and will accomplish nothing, but rather wait on the power of My contraction-unctions that will ripple through you yet again and again as the waves of the ocean. I will do this work through you, as you continually offer yourself to Me, as Mary did. Know that the warm oil of My Spirit will overflow you, enabling you to stretch and to push until you have birthed all of My latter-day purposes," promises your faithful Father.

Many years ago, the Lord gave the prophet Elijah the anointing and strength to travail and squat seven times on the mountain, birthing the rain in his day. Even so is the Father also empowering you now, dear Bride, to travail in this latter day. You will succeed, for have not His prophets prophesied the restoration of all things that will make way for the Lord's return?

The True Bride Found at the Well

Are you not, as John the Baptist, decreasing so that He might increase for the preparation of His soon return? This river is as a royal red carpet that is flowing down out of Heaven in preparation for the arrival of the great King of Kings and Lord of Lords. Indeed, this is a scarlet river flowing down from Calvary's cross so very long ago, offering new life to all those who will partake of it.

Did He not say that nations would come to the glorious, shimmering rivers of living water coming through you, beloved riverbed Bride? And even kings will be drawn to the brightness of your glorious rivers (see Isaiah 60:2-3). As He said long ago:

If any man is thirsty, let him come to Me and drink. He who believes in Me, as the Scripture said, "From his innermost being shall flow rivers of living water."
John 7:37-38

The True Bride Draws for Nations

Even as Abraham's servant asked for a fleece, a sign distinguishing Isaac's bride from the others, you must know, dear ones, that the Bride will be distinguished in this hour by her willingness to draw water for others. As Rebekah willingly drew, not only for the servant, but also offered to water all ten of his camels, even so is the true Bride today also freely offering to draw water for the multitudes of thirsty souls.

> "The bride will not be found among those who draw for themselves only," reminds the Father. "But she will be among those who will freely offer to draw for My many children, for the many thirsty souls of the tongues and tribes and peoples of all the nations of the earth."

The Well of Destiny

> "I am drawing you in this hour, My beloved, to the well of My living waters, just as I drew Rebekah to the well in Abraham's day. You must know that the well is where you will encounter your destiny and where you will be dispatched on your journey to meet your Bridegroom!"

In the Father's sovereignty, did He not cause Abraham's servant to stop for water at that well outside the city that day? And did He not send Rebekah at just the right moment to have an encounter with the master's servant, the one who would then lead her into her destiny, indeed even to meet her bridegroom, Isaac?

As the loving Father of all, is He not also the divine matchmaker in this late hour? The Father is sending His most esteemed Servant-Spirit to the four corners of the earth to fetch a glorious Bride for His faithful Son.

> "I am truly a jealous Father on behalf of My only begotten. I am causing the true Bride to thirst deeply in this hour, drawing her to My well yet

The True Bride Found at the Well

again and again and again. Are not My Spirit and Bride working and drawing together in this late hour?" asks the Father.

...the Spirit and the bride say, "Come." And let the one who hears say, "Come." And let the one who is thirsty come; let the one who wishes take the water of life without cost. Revelation 22:17

Amen!!

Endnotes:

1. Galatians 5:9.
2. See Matthew 5:6.
3. See Isaiah 60:2.

Chapter 5

Journey to the Bridegroom

Rebekah's brother Laban ran out to the well where Abraham's servant was. He saw the golden jewelry on his sister and heard her tell of the servant's words. He then invited the servant to come to their house to lodge, saying:

> *Come in, O blessed of the Lord! Why do you stand outside? For I have prepared the house, and a place for the camels.* Genesis 24:31, NKJ

The servant, his men and his camels lodged and ate with Laban, Rebekah and their family. Thus, the story of Abraham's commission to find a Bride for Isaac unfolds. The servant explains:

> *But he [Abraham] said to me, "The Lord, before whom I walk, will send His angel with you and prosper your*

way; and you shall take a wife for my son from my family and from my father's house."
                                    Genesis 24:40, NKJ

As the servant asks if Rebekah will come with him to become Isaac's bride, Laban and Bethuel answer:

...take her and go, and let her be your master's son's wife, as the Lord has spoken.
                                    Genesis 24:51, NKJ

When the servant heard these words, he bowed to the earth and worshipped God. Then the servant brought out many lavish gifts for Rebekah and her family:

Then the servant brought out jewelry of silver, jewelry of gold, and clothing, and gave them to Rebekah. He also gave precious things to her brother and to her mother.
                                    Genesis 24:53, NKJ

The servant and his men stayed the night, and in the morning, this conversation ensued:

He [the servant] said, "Send me away to my master." But her brother and her mother said, "Let the young woman stay with us a few days, at least ten; after that she may go."
And he said to them, "Do not hinder me, since the

Journey to the Bridegroom

> *Lord has prospered my way; send me away so that I may go to my master."*
> *So they said, "We will call the young woman and ask her personally."*
> *They then called Rebekah and said to her, "Will you go with this man?"*
> *And she said, "I will go."*
>
> Genesis 24:54-58, NKJ

Laban recognized Abraham's servant as being God's messenger and invited him in to lodge. Laban's welcome to the servant opened the door of divine blessing and destiny for his household, thereby forever changing the future of the entire family.

Will You Open the Door to the Holy Spirit?

> "Even so," says the Lord, "must My people, in this hour, be clear and discerning in recognizing Me and My latter-day purposes. Will you, My people, open the door of blessing and destiny for your households by welcoming My Spirit and My servants in this hour?" asks your Father. "Will you say to them: 'Come in, O Blessed of the Lord! Why do you stand outside? For I have prepared the house, and a place ... ?' "

The precious Servant, the most humble Holy Spirit, has been 'outside' for such a very long time. Will you invite Him in, calling Him, *"O Blessed of the Lord?"* Will you welcome all those who are with Him, who may be unfamiliar and even strange to you? Will you make practical and financial provision for His 'camels,' His vehicles or tools of the Gospel?

The Father-of-All, the Master, has an urgent and critical latter-day purpose — to fetch a glorious Bride for the awaiting Bridegroom. The Servant, the Holy Spirit, is knocking on the doors of hearts around the whole earth in this hour to find those who will welcome Him, His friends, and His gifts.

Will You Honor Him?

"Will you," asks the Lord, "hurry to honor and wash the feet of those I send to you? My Bride, you must always welcome My Spirit and whatever and whoever He brings for the day. You must choose to associate with those I send to you, even those who seem to be 'strangers from afar.' Your ears must be opened to the all-important message that is coming forth from My Spirit in this late hour.

"Will you listen to Him as He brings news from Heaven, where the Father-of-All is preparing for a wedding feast? Will you please not ignore Him, push Him aside, nor treat Him as your entertainment? You must stop using My precious Holy Spirit," warns the Lord, "to further your own kingdoms and to build your own empires.

> You must wake up and realize that you have an appointment with destiny. For this is not just another day, but this is the day of the ingathering and preparation of the Bride."

Unfortunately, there are many who will neither recognize nor follow His Spirit in this hour, thereby forfeiting their destiny, and forfeiting the all-important invitation to be taken to meet the Bridegroom. For what if Rebekah had refused Abraham's servant that day long ago? Very sadly, she would have forfeited forever her chance to be the wife of the master's son.

You Must Follow Quickly

You must know, beloved Bride, that when you encounter the Servant-Spirit in this hour, you must not only follow Him, but you must do so quickly. As Rebekah went out to the well that evening, just as she did every day, she had no idea that a stranger would meet her and insist on taking her — the very next morning — on a journey to meet her bridegroom. The entire course of her life was changed in a single moment.

There is no time to waste, honored Bride. Although Rebekah's family wanted to have her stay for ten more days before going with the servant, they consulted her and asked if she would be willing to go immediately, and she replied, *'I will go.'* You must be aware that the Father has sent out the Servant-Spirit to fetch you for the Bridegroom, and there is no time to waste. You must follow Him quickly in this hour and allow the Servant to take you on the journey that you have been waiting for all your life. The Master's Son, the Lamb-Bridegroom, has been waiting for such a very long time. Wedding preparations have begun!

Not an Easy Journey

"Dear Bride," says the Father, "I do not promise that this journey to meet your Bridegroom will be an easy or comfortable one. Instead, it promises to be long, hot and bumpy. Know that the pathway that leads to eternal life is narrow, and many will miss it. You may awake on the morning of your departure only to wonder what an illogical decision you have made. You will hear those around saying that you have lost your mind as you forsake all and follow My Servant to a land that you know not of. 'And why go in such a hurry?' they will say.

"Yes, your journey at times will be wearying, uncertain and lonely, as you singlemindedly betroth yourself to your Bridegroom. However, as you entrust yourself to the leading of My Servant, know assuredly that you will one day soon find yourself in the arms of your Beloved," promises your Father.

The Lord's abiding presence will journey with you, even as He was with Mary, who, being great with child, traveled to Bethlehem to fulfill her destiny. No, she was not comfortable either as she was compelled to follow destiny. It was neither comfort nor convenience that compelled Mary and Joseph to journey to that heavenly stable, the lowly birthplace of the King of Glory, while she was at the point of her delivery.

"Beloved Bride, are you not as Mary," asks your Father, "also journeying to follow destiny, while being great with My infant latter-day purposes? Even as I commissioned angels for Mary and Joseph's guidance and protection, know that I will also watch over you, protecting all that concerns you."

Beautified and Glorified

"Dear Bride, you will begin now to receive lavish end-time gifts of preparation and power," explains the Father. "Even as Abraham's servant honored Rebekah and her family with lavish gifts of gold and silver, so is the Servant-Spirit beginning now to take from Heaven's storehouse lavish end-time gifts for the glorification of the Bride."

Eye has not seen, nor ear heard,
Nor have entered into the heart of man

> *The things which God has prepared for those who love Him.*   1 Corinthians 2:9, NKJ

The Father is now searching hearts, to find the true Bride whose heart beats only to please her Bridegroom. As the Servant-Spirit finds the one who offers living water and who answers quickly, *"I will go,"* He begins to reach into Heaven's end-time storehouse of double-portion treasures and gifts, and He begins to prepare and adorn her for her Bridegroom.

Long ago, there was another bride who received lavish gifts of beautification for her wedding. The young woman Esther was favored and chosen to be the next queen by King Ahasuerus:

> *...the young woman pleased him, and she obtained his favor; so he readily gave beauty preparations to her, besides her allowance. Then seven choice maidservants were provided for her from the king's palace, and he moved her and her maidservants to the best place in the house of the women.*   Esther 2:9, NKJ

The first six months, she was prepared with the oil of myrrh, and then, for six more months, with perfumes and *"preparations for beautifying women"* (Esther 2:12, NKJ).

The last-day Bride is now in the period of her preparation and beautification, as was Esther preceding her union with King Ahasuerus.

"How much more will I, the King of Glory, who sits in the heavens, bestow lavish gifts of beautification and glorification upon My chosen Bride who pleases Me and finds favor with Me in this hour? Be assured My beloved, that I am sending forth My choice heavenly maidservants to attend to all the details of your preparation. I am sending the myrrh of My spirit of repentance and cleansing to deliver you from your spots, stains and wrinkles. And I am sending forth My latter-day refiner's fire through you yet again and again to prepare you for your jealous Bridegroom."

Beloved Bride, is not the heavenly perfume of His glory overtaking you yet more and more, causing you to swoon and become intoxicated with lovesickness while in His presence? Surely you are becoming more and more aware of His Spirit and of angels intervening in your daily lives in this late hour.

As you awaken each morning, is there not great anticipation in your spirit as you realize that the day of your wedding is fast approaching? As with any bride, you are becoming aware of so many things that have yet to be accomplished and prepared before the big day.

The Wedding Preparations

Perhaps you can see glimpses of the heavenly bridal preparations taking place behind the veil and curtains of the ordinary scenes and affairs of your daily lives? As you quiet yourselves and hear with the ear of your spirit, you may even hear the heavenly orchestras and choirs warming up in preparation for the celebration to come. Are you not more and more aware of the reality of the unseen in these last days?

The apostle John, on the island of Patmos, heard a voice from the throne saying:

Praise our God, all you His servants and those who fear Him, both small and great!
Let us be glad and rejoice and give Him glory, for the marriage of the Lamb has come, and His wife has made herself ready. And to her it was granted to be arrayed in fine linen, clean and bright, for the fine linen is the righteous acts of the saints.
Then he said to me [John], "Write: 'Blessed are those who are called to the marriage supper of the Lamb!"
... These are the true sayings of God!

Revelation 19:5 and 7-9, NKJ

As Abraham rightly explained to his servant that angels would prosper him in finding a bride, even so today are angels assisting the Holy Spirit in gathering and drawing the true Bride in this hour. Indeed, all the hosts of Heaven are passionately busying themselves with preparations for the event of all the ages.

The heavenly hosts are overcome with a holy awe as they are realizing how near the time is for the blessed

Journey to the Bridegroom

event. Royal, elegant tables are being set. Gowns and apparel are being created that is of a greater glory than anything ever witnessed upon the earth. The great cloud of witnesses is eagerly awaiting the final bit of time to tick away on the eternal time clock.

> "However," says the concerned Father, "there are many, many places left on the guest list that have not yet been confirmed. Therefore, I am sending forth the greater anointing in this hour to cast the net with greater effectiveness than ever before."

New Wine for the Wedding Feast

Is it not a sign that the Father of the Bridegroom is beginning to pour out the new wine in anticipation of the wedding? The joy of God's Spirit is truly being poured out upon the whole earth in this new day.

It was Jesus who first created wine for a wedding long ago. At the wedding in Cana of Galilee, the wine ran out, so Mary asked Jesus for help. He then requested the servants to fill six large waterpots with water:

> *And He said to them, "Draw some out now, and take it to the master of the feast." And they took it.*
> *When the master of the feast had tasted the water that was made wine, and did not know where it came from (but the servants who had drawn the water*

> *knew), the master of the feast called the bridegroom. And he said to him, "Every man at the beginning sets out the good wine, and when the guests have well drunk, then the inferior; You have kept the good wine until now!"* John 2:8-10, NKJ

Jesus' first miracle was creating wine for a wedding at His mother's request. One of the last great miracles will be (this time at the Father's request) providing the new wine for another wedding — the wedding of all the ages between the Lamb and His glorious Bride.

> "I have saved the best for last!" laughs the Father of all. "This wine has been aged for a very long time indeed, in preparation for this glorious season. This wine has been stored and saved in Heaven's winery, fermenting until just the right time — *'the appointed time to favor [Zion].'* " [1]

As the beloved Bride, we must understand that in the wedding of Cana, the waterpots were filled with ordinary water until they were poured out for the Master's use. It is imperative that we continually offer ourselves and our infillings to the Master, to be poured out according to His purposes. The Father is not looking for those who want to be saturated and full unto themselves, but for those who rejoice as Paul to be *"poured out as a drink offering on the sacrifice and service of [others'] faith"* (Philippians 2:17, NKJ).

The Lovesick Bride Longs for the Appearing of the Bridegroom

The Bridegroom-Son is not coming back for a bride who is dry and soberly self-focused, but rather He is returning for a well-saturated bride who is intoxicated with lovesickness for Him. The Bride, consumed with passion for her Bridegroom, cries out:

> *Like an apple tree among the trees of the woods,*
> *So is my beloved among the sons.*
> *I sat down in his shade with great delight,*
> *And his fruit was sweet to my taste.*
> *He brought me to the banqueting house,*
> *And his banner over me was love.*
> *Sustain me with cakes of raisins,*
> *Refresh me with apples,*
> *For I am lovesick.*
> *His left hand is under my head,*
> *And his right hand embraces me.*
>
> Song of Solomon 2:3-6, NKJ

The Bride, lovesick with passion and longing for her beloved Bridegroom, cries out with the Spirit, *"Come quickly!"* She cries out to the Root and Offspring of David, the Bright and Morning Star. She cries out to the One who was, who is, and who is to come. Her heart cries out to Him who is Faithful and True. She hungers for the Living Bread that came down out of Heaven, and in her darkness, she cries out for the True Light which enlightens every man.

The Bride cries out for the timeless Ancient of Days, for Him who is the same yesterday, today, and forever. She cries out for the gentle touch of the loving Shepherd of the sheep. In her need, she cries out for her Kinsmen Redeemer to cover her with that costly, scarlet blanket of love that was purchased at Calvary, even as Ruth was covered at the feet of Boaz so long ago. The Bride longs for that Fourth Man who appeared in the fiery furnace with Shadrach, Meshach and Abednego, the One whom even King Nebuchadnezzar recognized to be the Son of God.

The lovesick Bride welcomes the Bridegroom to come as the Consuming Fire and burn away all that is not of Him within her. Her warrior-heart calls out to the Captain of the Lord's Hosts whom Joshua encountered. Her heart cries out to the One that the prophet Malachi saw from afar, the Sun of Righteousness, who is even now arising to those who fear His name. She looks for the fierce, kingly Lion of the Tribe of Judah and for the gentle Lamb that was slain for the sins of the world. She looks for the One riding on the White Horse.

She seeks for the One who came to seek and to save the lost. She calls out to her High Priest, who understands her weakness and continually intercedes for her. Her bride-heart cries out to the One who is adorning her with the lavish gifts of the last days — the myrrh and perfume of His glory to prepare and beautify her.

The Bride adores the One who is the First and the Last, the living One, the One who has the keys of death and Hades. She cries out to the One John saw on the Island of Patmos, who stands tall in the midst of the seven lampstands, the seven churches:

One like a son of man, clothed in a robe reaching to the feet, and girded across His breast with a golden girdle. And His head and His hair were white like white wool, like snow; and His eyes were like a flame of fire; and His feet were like burnished bronze, when it has been caused to glow in a furnace, and His voice was like the sound of many waters. And in His right hand He held seven stars; and out of His mouth came a sharp two-edged sword; and His face was the like the sun shining in its strength. Revelation 1:13-20

Intimacy With the Bridegroom

The lovesick Bride longs to be embraced and swept into those strong arms that were willingly and lovingly stretched open wide for the sins of all, being nailed to the cross. She longs to be held by those arms that were wrapped around the whole world in the greatest love-sacrifice of all time. She longs to look closely into those fiery eyes, those eyes that can see all that is within her deepest heart, drawing her out of the shame and shadows of the past. She longs to swim deeply into those eyes of perfect love, never ever to leave.

She longs for the gentle caresses and touches of His hand, and she longs to feel and smell the fragrance of His life-breath surrounding her. She awakens morning by morning with Him on her mind, hoping He will visit throughout the day, spreading the garment of His precious presence around her, enveloping and adorning her with His rapturous glory. She longs to hear His sweet love-whispers in her deepest ear, and she longs to hear Him tell of the lavish gifts that He has prepared and reserved just for her. These glorious gifts have already been dispatched from eternity's prophetic storehouse and will be arriving daily, in double portion!

She longs to be intimate with Him, laying her head upon His bosom and hearing the beat of His heart. Becoming one with Him, feeling His heart of deep loving concern for the lost and hurting, she resolves to give herself more completely to His desires. She resolves to be even more possessed and consumed with His passions, to take the true Gospel with signs following to the ends of the earth, so that the end can come and He can return. She resolves to be a more effective 'riverbed,' welcoming greater and greater volumes of His living water to flow through her to all those who thirst, indeed to every tongue and tribe and people. She resolves to be a blessing to Israel, always praying for the peace of beloved Jerusalem. She resolves to bring healing and repair to the breaches so that all things would be restored, preparing the way of His soon return.

She looks for Him, she watches, she cries out:

Journey to the Bridegroom

Make haste, my beloved.
And be like a gazelle
Or a young stag
On the mountains of spices.

Song of Solomon 8:14, NKJ

The Bride says, "Come quickly, our Bridegroom-Lamb!"

The Love-Waltz of the Ages

As the great cloud of witnesses looks on, the greatest love-story of all time is unfolding. It was love unfathomable that caused the Father to offer His only Son as a sacrifice to buy back the world that He loved so much, thus creating the way for the multitudes of prodigals to find their way home. It was that same love that caused the Son to be willing to leave Heaven's glory, coming to those who would reject Him and send Him to Calvary's cruel cross. There He would become the sacrificial Lamb by becoming the curse, that many could inherit the blessing. The Bride has also been overcome with passionate love for her Bridegroom, and she is now offering herself for the Father's last-day purposes.

Perhaps you are able to hear Heaven's melody, the last-day waltz, as the Bridegroom steps forward onto the dance-floor of the end of the age, reaching for the Bride's hand? Never has her glory been so great, as she is embracing the Bridegroom, who is leading her in the greatest love-waltz of all the ages. The greatest courtship of all time is heating up!

The two are just beginning to dance in perfect harmony to the Father's last-day melody of mercy and deliverance for the nations. The Holy Spirit is falling upon the Bride's feet, anointing them to become as "hinds' feet," enabling her to follow the Bridegroom to those high places of glory:

The Lord God is my strength;
He will make my feet like deer's feet,
And He will make me walk on my high hills.
Habakkuk 3:19, NKJ

The Bride's feet have never been so beautiful as they are in these last days, as she takes His Good News to all:

How beautiful upon the mountains
Are the feet of him who brings good news,
Who proclaims peace,
Who brings glad tidings of good things,
Who proclaims salvation,
Who says to Zion,
"Your God reigns!" Isaiah 52:7, NKJ

The perfect couple, locked in rapturous embrace, is beginning to waltz over the hills and through the valleys, as they bring grace to all they encounter. Is this not the most incredible love-embrace ever imaginable, as the love between the Bride and the Bridegroom touches every nation and tongue and tribe of people? All who behold the couple are overcome with their glory, for as the bride follows the Bridegroom's lead, she is preparing the way of the Lord. As the cloud of glory begins to settle over their trail, we will begin to see:

Every valley shall be filled
And every mountain and hill brought low;
And the crooked places shall be made straight
And the rough ways made smooth;
And all flesh shall see the salvation of God.
Luke 3:5-6, NKJ

A Dowry of Many Souls

The love-smitten Bride is lifting high the name of her beloved Bridegroom so that many would be drawn to Him in this day of the great harvest. This last-day Bride will have the most unusual and most precious dowry of all time, for she will bring to Him many, many souls.

The Bride will not show up at the wedding of all the ages empty-handed, for she will bring billions of souls with her. Many are now catching glimpses of the Bridegroom as reflected in her love-smitten eyes. As she is beholding Him in His glory yet more and more, her eyes are filling with brilliant light, the Light of the World Himself! Multitudes upon multitudes living in darkness — even deep darkness — are being drawn to the powerful light beaming from the Bride. She is compelled to think and speak of Him daily, always honoring and lifting up His name so that many would be drawn to Him in this late hour. She has been completely overtaken with not only love for Him, but also with His love for souls!

Glory to the Lamb-Bridegroom! Amen!

Endnote:

1. Psalm 102:13, NKJ.

Chapter 6

It's Time to Build, Warriors

The God of Heaven will give us success:

Therefore we His servants will arise and build.
Nehemiah 2:20

We are entering into a season of building, the likes of which have never been seen. The Father has unrolled the blueprints of destiny, the last-day plans and strategies that will usher in the return of the Messiah. These blueprints and strategies are now being delivered and unveiled to those who have a heart to build according to the Father's desires.

The Father is looking for those who have a heart like that of Nehemiah, a man who, long ago, rebuilt the walls of Jerusalem. In his day, Nehemiah served as cupbearer to his king, King Artaxerxes of Babylon. He began to inquire about the welfare of his own brethren who lived in Jerusalem and discovered they were in a state of distress and reproach. As he prayed and fasted for their welfare, he was granted favor from his king, receiving both a leave of absence and the necessary resources to rebuild his beloved Jerusalem.

Let Us Rise Up and Build

As he supervised the building, Nehemiah addressed his fellow brethren, exhorting them:

> *You see the distress that we are in, how Jerusalem lies waste, and its gates are burned with fire. Come and let us build the wall of Jerusalem, that we may no longer be a reproach.* Nehemiah 2:17, NKJ

Nehemiah encouraged his brethren by testifying, "The good hand of the Lord is upon me." And so must we, as the last-day brethren, be encouraged, as we begin to realize that 'the good hand of the Lord' is once again upon us, His people! He is sending His double anointing to war with one hand and to build and restore with the other hand. Let us, as last-day Nehemiahs, declare, *"Let us rise up and build"* (Nehemiah 2:18, NKJ). We must, as our courageous forefathers before us, put our hands to the good work.

"This is truly the day of My building," says the God of Nehemiah. "I am, today, rebuilding the borders of My people, Zion, as I am regathering them from the uttermost parts of the earth as a hen gathers her chicks to herself. I am rebuilding the walls, repairing the breaches, and hanging the gates of My beloved Zion. You haven't seen anything yet, My people, compared to what will soon be revealed.

"I am preparing and adorning the Bride to become the glorious wife of the Lamb-Bridegroom, for I am building as I have never built before in history. I am creating and building the great last-day net for the massive harvest of souls that is beginning to come in. This is, indeed, the season of preparation, of restoration, and of harvest," explains the Father-Engineer.

"And I am now placing upon many of you in this hour the mantle of Nehemiah. I will place on you the spirit of loving concern for the welfare of your brethren. I will mantle you with the wisdom and leadership that is necessary to begin to rebuild the walls around My people, Zion."

Builders Receive Favor

"Even as Nehemiah, in his day, received favor from his king, so will I today, as your King, favor you, My latter-day warrior-builders, for the rebuilding of the walls of My people," says the

Lord. "First, I will set your hearts on fire for your brethren that are suffering reproach. Indeed, I will give to you My very own heart concerning them and their welfare.

"I will then provide you with all the resources, both natural and spiritual, that you will need for the rebuilding of the walls. Continually look to Me, the Master Builder, for your blueprints and instructions. Remember that you are restoring *"the city ... whose architect and builder is God."* [1] This is that city that cannot be built with the arm of the flesh nor by the carnal mind, but only in the power of My Spirit and Word. This is that city that many longed to see, and you have the honor and the privilege to build it and to fight for it, My last-day warriors."

A Double Mantle: Build and Fight

"Receive your mantle of Nehemiah and receive a heart of love and compassion for the welfare of your brethren. Receive My favor in this hour, and trust Me to provide you with the abundance of resources you will need to build; for this one's on Me!" laughs your faithful Father. "Receive from Me the spirit of holy courage and strength to build in the face of your persistent enemies.

"Just as Nehemiah received a double-portion mantle to build and to fight at the same time,

It's Time to Build, Warriors

so is this double-portion mantle now available to you, as you rise up to meet this divine challenge. As Tobiah and Sanballat, the enemies of Jerusalem, were enraged when they heard of the work of rebuilding, so are your enemies enraged today because they see the walls are beginning to be rebuilt, and they know their time is very short indeed. Yes, they will blaspheme and mock you today, too, as you build My Kingdom. They will seek to frighten and intimidate you, but you must exhort one another as did My servant Nehemiah:

" *'Do not be afraid of them. Remember the Lord, great and awesome, and fight for your brethren, your sons, your daughters, your wives, and your houses.'*
Nehemiah 4:14, NKJ

"My warriors, you must realize that your own welfare is not the only issue; your sons, daughters, spouses, indeed your entire families are at stake. Passivity and complacency have crept in like thieves in the night, so you must rouse yourselves, pick up your spiritual weapons, and begin to fight and build again. Do not focus on the comfort and security of your circumstances which are temporal, but begin to strengthen yourselves by focusing on the issues of My Kingdom — on the eternal welfare of those around you."

A Wise Man Builds Upon the Rock

"You must remind yourself frequently that eternity is at hand, and that all else will soon perish. Many of you take great care to store up and invest for your futures, and rightly so, My people. But you must keep in mind that eternity is only one heartbeat away for the multitudes upon multitudes of people that inhabit the earth. The primary thing on My Father's heart in this hour is to throw open wide the ark-door of salvation, drawing many from every tongue and tribe into My eternal family. You must understand that, as a father, I am concerned for the welfare of each of My many children. I am searching the ends of the earth for willing and obedient ark builders who will build according to My Spirit and My Word."

Let us heed the words of the apostle Paul, a wise and experienced master builder who laid much of the foundation of the early Church:

For we are God's fellow workers; you are God's field, you are God's building.
According to the grace of God which was given to me, as a wise master builder I have laid the foundation, and another builds on it. But let each one take heed how he builds on it. For no other foundation can any-

> *one lay than that which is laid, which is Jesus Christ. Now if anyone builds on this foundation with gold, silver, precious stones, wood, hay, straw, each one's work will become clear; for the Day will declare it, because it will be revealed by fire; and the fire will test each one's work, of what sort it is.*
> *If anyone's work which he has built on it endures, he will receive a reward. If anyone's work is burned, he will suffer loss; but he himself will be saved, yet so as through fire.*   1 Corinthians 3:9-15, NKJ

Do you remember the parable of the foolish man who built his house upon the sand and the wise man who built his house upon the rock (see Matt. 7:24-28)? The winds and the storms came and beat upon both houses, and the house that was built upon the rock stood strong, but the house that was built upon the sand was destroyed.

> "I exhort you, My children, seek first My Kingdom and invest in the limitless treasures that shall last forever. As you listen to Me intently in this late hour, obeying quickly, you will be established upon the Rock, upon Jesus, the Chief Cornerstone, Who will never be shaken nor removed. Truly the last-day storms and winds shall come, but know that as you hide yourself in Me and in My purposes, you shall surely be sustained and protected," promises your faithful Father.

The Wall of Unity, Prayer and Authority

Surely the walls surrounding God's people have been broken down, thus allowing the enemy access. But just as in the days of Nehemiah, there was an appointed time for the walls to be rebuilt, so this is your appointed time, Zion. It is time for a corporate wall to be built, for this alone will provide protection and refuge from the continual onslaught of enemy forces.

The living stones shall be made into a wall of unity as the supernatural love of God joins them together. This corporate wall is being formed through the networking of prayer and intercession in a way that has never been before. The watchmen and intercessors shall link arms and hearts in such a way as to form an impenetrable barrier to the enemy. The prayer movement that has begun will continue to grow in both volume and intensity, crescendoing into ever-increasing waves of power that will cover the earth. Prayer relationships will develop with those in close proximity, but there will also be a bonding between those of different regions and countries.

The wall also represents the true emerging leaders of the Body of Christ, especially the last-day apostles and prophets. As the old religious system, 'the Saul order,' continues to be uprooted and removed, the leaders of the Davidic order will emerge. The mantle of the kingship of Jesus Himself will rest upon these meek and anointed ones who have been reserved for this hour. The world has never seen such as these warrior-leader-builders!

These leaders will shepherd the flock with the heart

of God, bringing healing to many prodigals. They will serve with grace and lead with wisdom and maturity. As these leaders emerge, we will begin to see true victory for the Body of Christ. These leaders will begin to deal authoritatively and effectively with the onslaughts of the enemy against the flock. As the gaps in the walls are closed and the gates are hung, it will be much more difficult to gain access to the flock.

"I Am Breaking the Mold"

But we must understand that before this corporate wall of protection can be constructed, the existing walls of division and disunity must first be torn down and removed. A wall of unity cannot be constructed upon a wall of disunity. We must yield to the Lord and cooperate with Him as He destroys these strongholds of misunderstanding, mistrust and forced conformity.

Long ago, when the children of Israel were enslaved by the taskmasters of Egypt, they were forced to create bricks. The bricks had to be uniform, each one exactly the same, with no differences or variance. If the slaves did not conform to the desire of the leaders, they felt the whip lashed against their backs. The slaves were required to fashion images of their leaders, of the Pharaohs who ruled over them by force.

> "It is the same taskmaster spirit of slavery and legalism," explains the concerned Father, "that continues to lash against the living stones of My

people today, forcing them into conformity. Indeed, religious taskmasters have required that each living stone meet their specifications, conforming to their needs and whims, to their visions and to their personalities.

"This harsh spirit has been like the stonemason's chisel, cutting very deeply into the heart of My people. It has caused even some of My strongest and mightiest of warriors to become disheartened and disillusioned. It has caused some to forget their all-important destiny, and even who they are," grieves the Father.

"Know, My children, that the relentless pounding of the religious chisel that requires you to be clones of your leaders is not from Me. Immature leaders and those overtaken with the spirits of control, religion, and legalism, delight in hammering all their subjects into boxes, into the places that will best serve and protect their interests. But the true leaders I am now raising up will have My heart; they will celebrate the vast diversity of My many children and the gifts and treasures I have placed within them. I am raising up leaders who are secure in their relationship with Me, and they will yield to My Spirit as He leads through them."

It's Time to Build, Warriors

The Father Fashions a Glorious Bride Mosaic

The immature and insecure leaders who have self-serving agendas delight in uniformity, where everything and everyone is easily manageable and under their control. However, know that the true building that is being created by God's Spirit is infinitely diverse, resembling a glorious mosaic, where each member, each living stone, is lovingly hand carved and placed by the Father Himself. Each living stone will be displayed, celebrated and honored for its uniqueness and splendor. The whole will become an image, or a reflection, of the infinite vastness, diversity and glory of the Father Himself.

Whereas the slaves of Egypt were forced to create images of the Pharaoh-overseers who ruled over them, God's many children today, His many living stones, are willingly offering themselves to become a part of the Father's masterbuilding and to become a reflection of *His* image.

> "The true walls of My heavenly dwelling," says the Father-Designer, "are built of many separate and diverse living stones. These stones are merged into a glorious bride-mosaic through the love-mortar of the blood sacrifice of the Lamb." [2]

The Father Is Avenging His Body

The Master Stonecarver Himself is now delivering His children from the harsh and destructive chisel-spirits of religion, control and legalism. The Father has released a new and greater anointing, the spirit of Elijah, to confront and destroy these evil powers that have counterfeited His leadership. The same spirit that was upon Elijah the prophet long ago to confront and destroy the wickedness of Ahab and Jezebel is now being poured out in double portion upon God's faithful leaders. The Father is avenging His Body, and will continue to expose and burn these dark forces from their roots up (see Malachi 4:1).

But children, know that you must cooperate with Him in your deliverance. He has warned you in His Word (see Colossians 2 and Galatians 3) that you must not submit yourselves to these influences. Their power is now being broken by the Spirit, but you must turn and walk away from them, and search out those humble leaders who are representing the real Jesus, the true Head of the Body. The Lord's true leaders have a balance of strength and meekness, with the Father's heart of love for the sheep. When you see the Father's image reflected in the people, rather than the leaders' image, you will know that The Son, the kind and good Shepherd, is in charge.

The Father Re-Excavates Faulty Foundations

"Yes, My children, you must understand that I cannot build upon crooked foundations. Therefore, I am in the process of excavation right now, digging up and removing foundational walls that are in conflict with My purposes and My ways. It will surely be messy for awhile; the dust will

It's Time to Build, Warriors

fly as I sort through the age-old foundations of My people!

"Through the merciful bright light of My Spirit, I will search out foundational attitudes and beliefs in My people that are contrary to My nature. Again, I challenge you to yield to Me and cooperate with Me so that I can remove these stumbling blocks that are in the way of your progress. And yes, My dear ones, some of these stumbling blocks are in your very own hearts and minds."

The stumbling blocks and barriers that have come as a result of denominationalism, racism and gender prejudices are being annihilated. Just as a wise and caring dentist removes a bad tooth, so is the Father in the process of removing bad root attitudes and wrong beliefs from His Bride. As He shines His light on these things, we must be willing to see the truth and repent and let go of them. We must continue to welcome the renewing and cleansing of our minds and hearts. Indeed, for each living stone to be placed into the eternal wall, it must reflect the character and nature of the Lamb who purchased it.

The Chief Cornerstone Set in Place

Be comforted in knowing that the Father is the Architect and Builder of this eternal wall and dwelling (see Hebrews 11:10). When Jesus, the Chief Cornerstone

Himself, came to earth two thousand years ago, the builders rejected Him (see Luke 20:17). But the Master Architect has not changed His original plans, for the foundation that He has laid no man can change.

"And as you build according to My blueprints, My last-day warrior-builders," says the Father, "the Chief Cornerstone will, at last, take His honored position, a position that will not be rejected this time.

"As Isaiah the prophet saw so long ago:

" *'For a child will be born to us, a son will be given to us;*
And the government will rest on His shoulders;
And His name will be called Wonderful Counselor, Mighty God,
Eternal Father, Prince of Peace.
There will be no end to the increase of His government or of peace,
On the throne of David and over his kingdom,
To establish it and to uphold it with justice and righteousness
From then on and forevermore.' Isaiah 9:6-7

Stay on the Wall

"My people, do not be concerned or surprised at the enemy's attacks, for have I not said that

It's Time to Build, Warriors

he is the accuser of the brethren and the father of lies? Yes, he will persistently and ruthlessly conspire against you, but you will prevail and overcome him by listening intently to My voice of instructions and by obeying quickly.

"He will attempt to stop the work of rebuilding every way he can, through temptations, and he may even send false prophets, as he sent to Nehemiah in his day. Do not allow the enemy to pull you off the wall, for that is exactly what he wants. Beware of his strategies and realize he is bent on wearing down the saints during this critical hour of restoration. [3] Keep your ears tuned to the life-voice of your Captain, while building with one hand and fighting with the other, as I am now empowering you with this last-day double mantle," exhorts your Father.

"It is imperative that you focus on your assignment, My warrior-builders, for there is more riding on your success than you can imagine. It will not be easy to stay focused on your tasks, because there will be many distractions and disturbances around you. However, you must be diligent to walk with Me closely and listen to My voice intently. You must listen not only to the voice of the Master Builder, but also to the voice of the Commander of Armies, so I can unfold to you, battle by battle, My strategies for victory. Through My prophetic voice, you will have a hotline of divine intelligence linking you to My heavenly throne-room headquarters. Have I not placed watchmen on your walls, O Zion? My people, listen to them!"

Our God Will Fight for Us!

"Do not be independent in this hour, but find your place on the wall. I will give you specific instructions as you seek Me, showing you where to build and what to do. Know that you have been formed, fashioned and equipped for the destiny that you are now stepping into."

As Nehemiah exhorted his brethren, we too must set up a guard for both day and night, and sound the trumpet to rally to one another as needed to cover and protect the lower and exposed places:

At whatever place you hear the sound of the trumpet, rally to us there. Our God will fight for us.
Nehemiah 4:20

"Build and fight," challenges the Lord, "this is truly the hour for My warriors to build and to fight. Give yourselves, as never before, to this work of restoration, for Heaven must retain Jesus until the restoration of all things. [4] There are many, many POW's who are awaiting release,

It's Time to Build, Warriors

waiting for someone clothed in the resurrection power of Jesus Himself, to come and blast open their prison doors.

"And yes, know assuredly that I will fight for you as you build for Me, according to My instructions. I will cover and protect you in this day of My vengeance," promises your Father, "for I have much to accomplish."

Cities of Refuge

"There are many cities of refuge that need to be constructed," pleads the Father, "so that I will have places to bind up the wounded and heal the brokenhearted. I am pouring out much grace in this hour, My people, but I need containers and structures that I can pour this grace into so that it can be easily available to the masses who desperately need it. I have begun this work, but there is much left to be done. In fact, I have already begun what will become prototypes for other centers. I am wanting to create cities of refuge in every region, so they will be readily available to those who have need of them.

"I desire to raise up centers of healing, deliverance and provision," explains the Father. "It is not enough for the wounded and the needy to attend services, they need to have a place to live and to be loved and restored to wholeness and strength. They need a place to be discipled in how to live daily life in an overcoming way. I desire to manifest to these in need not only preaching of the truth, but the truth lived out in daily life, in daily relationships, in marriages and in families. As these broken ones come into wholeness and knowledge, they will, in turn, become mighty warriors who will have great anointing and wisdom to share with others."

Each One Will Be Unique

As leaders of each region inquire of the Lord, He will begin to unfold to them the masterplan for their geographical area. Each center will be designed according to its region's unique characteristics and needs. These centers will be hospitals for sick bodies, sick souls and sick families. The Lord will pour out supernatural signs and wonders as never before, but He also desires to impart knowledge and wisdom in stewarding the wholeness He is giving to them.

The earth is coming into the deep darkness that Isaiah the prophet saw long ago (see Isaiah 60:2). These God-ordained centers will become beacons of light, even massive lighthouses, shining forth the light of His glory, guiding individuals and families into the safe harbor of His love. He is calling for builders to construct and support hospital-lighthouses, which will

It's Time to Build, Warriors

house those who need to see His love and mercy manifested in practical and tangible ways.

> "I want to offer food to the hungry, clothes for the naked, comfort and healing for the sick," says the compassionate Father. "I want to pour out My delivering power to set the captives free. And finally, I want to impart destiny and purpose into the hearts of those who are in despair.
>
> "Who will build with Me and for Me?" asks the Father of mercy. "Who will yield to Me and labor with Me in this all-important mission?"

These centers, these cities of mercy and refuge, will become like an oasis in the midst of a desert. And know that the life and mercy poured out to those in need will be shared by those who co-labor with Him.

Even as the prophet Haggai in his day exhorted the people to build, so are we being exhorted to build:

> *Be strong ...and work for I am with you ... . According to the word that I covenanted with you when you came out of Egypt, so My Spirit remains among you; do not fear! Once more (it is a little while) I will shake heaven and earth .... And they shall come to the Desire of All Nations, and I will fill this temple with glory. The silver is Mine and the gold is Mine. The glory of this latter temple shall be greater than the former.*   Haggai 2:4-9, NKJ

"I Need Bridgebuilders"

"I am needing bridgebuilders in this hour who will bring together My two beloved peoples, Israel and the 'Gentile' or 'Christian' Church. This is the hour of reconciliation, My dear ones. Yes, there has been much misunderstanding and distance between the two, but I am now bringing them together, even as two highways are merged into one. Even as you are traveling down destiny's highway, as you seek Me, you will see roadsigns in My Word telling you to move to the left or to the right.

"You are traveling into a new place, a place never before traveled. As you listen to the still small voice of My Spirit, you will be guided into new realms of destiny and glory, accomplishing all that has been prophesied for the end," explains the Father.

"I am forming new relationships between My people Israel and the Church. These relationships that are born of My Spirit will form the 'cross ties' on the last-day 'train track.' Each relationship will form another cross tie that will lengthen the track, bringing it farther into the fulfillment of My purposes.

It's Time to Build, Warriors

"Be obedient in this hour, My people. Yield to My Spirit in everything, for every decision and relationship is important now. Each cross tie is necessary to enable both sides of the track to be completed, enabling this train of greater anointing to travel to the nations of the earth."

Parallel Tracks: Israel and the Church

This outpouring of restoration, this Holy Ghost and fire train, will travel down the prophetic tracks of the parallel restoration of the Church and of Israel — double restoration. This glory train will be pulling many great and diverse mantles of anointing throughout the whole earth for the accomplishment of the Father's purposes in this late hour.

"My double-portion Spirit will restore the Church, and My people Israel," says the Lord, "for the two are eternally interconnected and interrelated. Did I not say to Abraham that all the families of the earth would be blessed in him? [5] For I have not forgotten My covenant with My chosen. I am reminding the Church in this hour:

" *'Remember that you do not support the root, but the root supports you.'* Romans 11:18, NKJ

" *'For I do not desire, brethren, that you should be ignorant of this mystery, lest you should be wise in your*

own opinion, that blindness in part has happened to Israel until the fullness of the Gentiles has come in.'
Romans 11:25, NKJ

"Even as a train cannot go down a one-sided track, even so the Church cannot go ahead of My servant Israel," explains the Father. "And Israel, neither can you run ahead of the Christian Church. I am calling for My builders, those anointed with wisdom and strength, to lay the track, step by step, beam by beam, and relationship by relationship.

"You will enter into your inheritance together as both sides of the track are built, so that My glory train of the Gospel — with signs and wonders following — may truly run through every mountain and valley where all the tongues and tribes and peoples of the earth dwell. You must work and build together, My people, as never before in history," exhorts the Father. [6]

Endnotes:

1. Hebrews 11:10.
2. See 2 Peter 2:5.
3. See Daniel 7:25.
4. See Acts 3:21.
5. See Genesis 12:3.
6. The topic of reconciliation between Israel and the Christian Church is both challenging and involved. I would like to refer readers to a very fine book entitled *Mysteries of the Glory Unveiled* by David Herzog (Hagerstown, MD, McDougal Publishing: 2000), which provides an excellent summary of this very important issue. In the book's last chapter, "A Return to Our Roots," David provides an informative, but easy-to-understand overview. A must read! For those who want more study on this subject, I suggest you visit the website: www.MessianicJewish.net or call (800) 410-7367 for a catalog of related literature.

Chapter 7

And Your Whole House Shall Be Saved

During these critical last days the Father is searching for those who are able to discern the times. He is searching for those who will be used as faith catalysts for the saving of entire families.

The Father is searching for those who will follow the example of a woman named Rahab who lived long ago. She and her family were not of the lineage of faith, but when her moment of destiny arrived, she was able to discern the times and save herself and her family.

Rahab Recognizes the One True God

After the death of Moses, Joshua sent out two spies to secretly view the land of Jericho. The two spies lodged in the house of Rahab, who lived on the wall of the city. When the king of Jericho heard of the spies coming to Rahab's house, he requested that she send them out. But she lied to the king, telling him that they had already left, when in fact she had hidden them on the roof among stalks of flax. After the king's men left, Rahab went up to the roof and spoke to the spies;

> *I know that the Lord has given you the land, that the terror of you has fallen on us, and that all the inhabitants of the land are fainthearted because of you. For we have heard how the Lord dried up the water of the Red Sea for you when you came out of Egypt, and what you did to the kings of the Amorites who were on the other side of the Jordan, Sihon and Og, whom you utterly destroyed. And as soon as we heard these things, our hearts melted; neither did there remain any courage in anyone because of you, for the Lord your God, He is God in heaven above and on earth beneath.* Joshua 2:9-11, NKJ

The Father Is Searching for Rahabs

Even as Joshua sent out the two spies to Jericho, so the Father is now sending His Spirit to spy out the land, looking for present-day Rahabs who will recognize Him as the One true living God that He is and declare, *"for the Lord your God, He is God!"*

He is looking for those with a heart of courage who will defy the edicts of the 'kings' of this day, putting their lives on the line to cover and protect His purposes. He is looking for latter-day warriors who have the spiritual discernment and good sense to seize the op-

And Your Whole House Shall Be Saved

portunity, realizing that the battle of the ages is just beginning.

He is looking for those who will beseech Him to make covenant with them, not only for themselves, but for their entire households. He is searching for those who will cry out to Him today, as Rahab cried out to the spies in her day:

Now therefore, I beg you, swear to me by the Lord, since I have shown you kindness, that you also will show kindness to my father's house, and give me a true token, and spare my father, my mother, my brothers, my sisters, and all that they have, and deliver our lives from death. Joshua 2:12-13, NKJ

The spies answered Rahab by saying:

Our lives for yours ... . We will be blameless of this oath of yours which you have made us swear, unless, when we come into the land, you bind this line of scarlet cord in your window ... , and unless you bring your father, your mother, your brothers, and all your father's household to your own home.
Joshua 2:14 and 17-19, NKJ

A Lamb for Each Household

It was no accident, Zion, that the cord in Rahab's window, the sign of her covenant with Joshua, was a scarlet cord. It was a picture of the delivering, rescuing power of the precious blood that would be shed on Calvary so many years later, a foreshadowing of the New Covenant, through which divine rescue would be offered to all mankind. The blood is the scarlet cord, even the scarlet lifeline, thrown down out of Heaven, out of the Father's heart of love and mercy, offering a way of escape to all who will lay hold of it. The veil between God and all men was forever torn and removed, based on the shedding of the blood of His Son Jesus. He was the onetime Sacrifice for all who would believe, providing divine-rescue from sure and eternal destruction.

Did not Joshua and his spies recall how, more than forty years earlier, another divine rescue had taken place for the children of Israel as they escaped Egypt? The doorposts and lintels of their homes were marked by the scarlet covenant of blood, even the blood of a lamb, through the command of Moses. Each family was instructed to take one lamb for each household, insuring their protection from the death angel and promising their deliverance from slavery.

> "Through Calvary's sacrifice, I am now, as the Father-of-All, providing the-Lamb-that-was-slain to cover each and every household with its delivering, rescuing power. If I made covenant with Noah, Abraham and the children of Israel before the shedding of My Son's blood, how much more will I, in this day, honor those who are painting His blood, the blood of the New Covenant, not only over themselves, but over all

And Your Whole House Shall Be Saved

those in their families as well," promises your faithful Father.

The God of Families

"Am I not the God of families? Am I not the One who created Father Adam and Mother Eve, giving them power to birth and rear children, creating mankind in families? As a Father, My desire was to establish a great family so that we could all be together forever. Know most assuredly that I plan to bless and establish families in this late hour."

"In Noah's day, I revealed Myself as the God of family covenant, as I rescued not only him, but also his entire family. And when I made covenant with Rahab, did I not promise to show mercy to all those of her family whom she brought under her roof? When I established My covenant with Abraham, those who received its blessings were his very own family members — Sarah his wife, his son Isaac and his grandson Jacob."

The grace and protection of God's covenant with Abraham extended to his nephew Lot, even while he was living in Sodom and Gomorrah. Did God not send two angels to lodge with Lot and his family, warning them of imminent destruction? Yes, His rescue was mercifully offered to every member of Lot's family, even to the sons-in-law who refused, thinking it was a joke. And when Lot, his wife, and daughters lingered the morning of judgment, angels took them by the hands and led them out, placing them outside the city and giving them instructions for their protection.

Even as the Lord sent angel messengers to Lot and his family because of His covenant with Abraham, so is He sending His Messenger-Spirit in this hour to offer rescue to all those in our households. His merciful spirit of preparation, the spirit of Elijah, is beginning to be poured out in this day, *"before the coming of the great and dreadful day of the Lord"* (Malachi 4:5, NKJ). His Spirit is hovering over those households that are covered with the Lamb's blood, His Spirit always honoring the blood covenant.

> "I challenge you, My people," says the God of Covenant, "to take the hyssop of your faith and appropriate the blood of My Son over your entire households, as Rahab covenanted with Joshua by tying the scarlet cord in her window so long ago. Even as the two spies exhorted her to bring all those of her family into her house for their protection, so am I, in this day, exhorting My faithful children to appropriate the Lamb's blood over all their households by faith, trusting in the God of covenant."

And Your Whole House Shall Be Saved

Warriors File in Rank

The two spies in Rahab's day were forerunners, a sign to those around that Joshua and his army were indeed on the way. Even so, today, is the spirit of Elijah also a forerunner, a sign to all who can see and hear, that God is preparing troops for battle. Even as the spies were sent out together as a twosome, a 'double-team', so is the Lord sending out His Spirit in double portion to spy out and overtake the Jerichos of these latter days.

Rahab daily checked the scarlet cord in her window, making certain that it was secure. She watched out her window, eagerly awaiting Joshua and the mighty warriors who would rescue her and her family.

> "It is time now, My people," says the Lord, "to go to the window of your hearts to watch for your Joshua-Jesus, who is now sending His powerful Warrior-Spirit ahead to prepare you for the challenging days ahead.

> "As you look out the faith window of your hearts, can you see glimpses of My mighty army rallying together? My latter-day warriors are beginning to find their place and march in rank around the latter-day Jerichos that are defying the armies of the living God in this day. If you look closely, you will see the fiery vengeance in their eyes and the brilliance of My light reflecting off their breastplates and shields. You may

be almost blinded by the glory of My Word, as it comes forth from their hearts and mouths as two-edged swords," explains the King of Glory.

The Lamb's Surrender Becomes the Lion's Triumph

If we listen carefully, we will hear the sound of adoring praise and worship for the Lamb rolling over the hills and thundering through the valleys, as last-day warriors gather and march. We may even hear the sound of a mighty roar echoing throughout the land, as of a kingly Lion-Commander who is beginning to reclaim His territory and His warrior-bride. As we focus on the spiritual horizon, we will be able to see troops that are beginning to march around latter-day Jerichos day by day, even as Joshua commanded his priest-troops to do for seven days.

Joshua commanded the people to be silent the first six days around the city, waiting for that final victory shout on the seventh day (see Joshua 6:10). They were foreshadowing the Lamb who would later march around the stronghold of sin and death, enduring His suffering in silence:

> *He was led as a sheep to the slaughter;*
> *And like a lamb before its shearers is silent,*
> *So He opened not His mouth.*   Acts 8:32, NKJ

And did Jesus, the High-Priestly-Warrior of all time,

And Your Whole House Shall Be Saved

not also march seven times around every stronghold and every Jericho that would defy us?

Having disarmed principalities and powers, He made a public spectacle of them, triumphing over them in it.
Colossians 2:15, NKJ

Yes, He suffered as the Lamb-Priest who was led to the slaughter, shedding His blood seven ways, thereby completing the work of redemption and rescue for all who would ever call upon His precious name. That sinless Great Warrior marched around the sin and death of the whole world even the seventh time, triumphing forever as He sounded that final victory shout *"it is finished"* from a lonely hill called Golgotha. He thus proclaimed eternal triumph to all those who would ever receive it. The resounding roar of His victory shout shook even Hell itself, echoing and reverberating throughout every dark corridor as He took captivity captive, reclaiming the keys of death and Hell forever (see Revelation 1:18). The Lamb's surrender three days later became the Lion's triumph as He burst forth out of the tomb that could not hold Him!

Warrior-Priests Marching the Seventh Time

And was this Lamb-Warrior not the firstborn of many? And do you not see the many beginning now to file in rank along behind Him, marching to His orders?

You will see these latter-day warriors, young and old alike, paying the ultimate price, losing their lives daily for the sake of their beloved Lion-Commander. You will see them quietly, but determinedly, receiving and carrying out their Commander's orders each and every day. These are the dreaded latter-day warriors that have but one passion in life, following the Lamb wherever He leads, loving not their own lives even unto death, and eagerly pouring themselves out for the faith of others.

As we turn our eyes toward the spiritual horizon of this last day, we may catch a glimpse of the great army that Ezekiel saw so long ago, being formed and connected joint-to-joint and bone-to-bone. We may hear the noise of a mighty rattling in the Spirit as they are coming together, and we may even feel the very life-breath of God Himself, as the four winds of His Spirit prophesy and breathe upon the dead bones, bringing life to Zion, creating *"an exceedingly great army"* (Ezekiel 37:10, NKJ).

> "Are you not awakening morning by morning to the smell and sound of war in this late hour?" inquires your Warrior-Father. "Surely you are feeling a stirring and restlessness in your spirit, as destiny beckons you day by day to rise up and watch for your beloved Lion-Commander as He is reclaiming His warrior-bride. You were indeed born for such a time as this, My great last-day champions," exhorts your loving Father.

And Your Whole House Shall Be Saved

"Are you able to discern that these warriors are beginning now to march around last-day Jerichos for *the seventh* time? You must understand that this last march around will be the great battle of the ages. Indeed, it is this last march around that *will eventually* close the age.

"Listen closely and you will hear the dreaded warriors declaring *"it is finished"* to the last-day strongholds that have withstood My purposes, echoing Jesus' eternal victory cry from Calvary so long ago. Know that you will begin to see the walls of latter-day Jerichos shake, rattle, and roll under divine pressure as My greater anointing of power is poured out in this hour upon My faithful warrior-priests," promises your jubilant Father.

Time to Watch

Are you like Rahab, excitedly pacing back and forth, going to the window of your heart to look for your Joshua-Jesus and His warrior-Spirit, yet again, and again, and again?

"Know, My people, that this is the appointed day of rescue for you and your families, as I have sent forth My Spirit to prepare you for My soon return.

"I am sending My mighty Warrior-Spirit in this day to prepare and rescue latter-day Rahabs and their households. You can be assured that I will honor the blood of My very own Son that has been painted over the doorposts of your families with the hyssop of your faith and faithfulness to Me," promises the God-of-Covenant.

Are you like Rahab, watching from the window of your heart, searching for your Joshua-Jesus? Are you welcoming His Commander-Spirit, who has been sent to prepare the troops for battle?

And Your Whole House Shall Be Saved

For Jesus answered and said to them [His disciples], "Indeed, Elijah is coming first and will restore all things." Matthew 17:11, NKJ

The spirit of Elijah is coming to prepare the way for the Lord's return, even as John the Baptist prepared the way for the Lord's coming. The angel Gabriel appeared to the priest Zacharias as he was in the Temple burning incense long ago, according to the custom of the priesthood. Gabriel explained to him that he would be the father of one called John. The angel explained to Zacharias the purpose for which John was to be born:

And he [John] will turn many of the children of Israel to the Lord their God. He will also go before Him in the spirit and power of Elijah, 'to turn the hearts of the fathers to the children,' and the disobedient to the wisdom of the just, to make ready a people prepared for the Lord. Luke 1:16-17, NKJ

Latter-Day Rahabs, Let's Make Covenant

O Lord, we receive and honor the blood of Jesus, spreading it forth as a scarlet blanket of grace over our entire households in this late hour. Through the hyssop of our prayer of faith, we appropriate the blood of the Lamb over all those in our families, just as Rahab of old gathered her family under the refuge of the covenant of the scarlet rope in her window. We welcome and honor You, precious Holy Spirit, through Your great latter-day anointing, to enlighten all those in our households to the saving and rescuing power of Jesus' blood.

Come and cleanse, deliver and prepare our households for the days ahead, merciful Father, even as in Moses' day, when You brought out all the people — both the young and the old and all in between. So we thank You, faithful Father, for the offer of grace You are extending to all those in our families in this late hour.

We look out the faith-windows of our hearts and spirits daily, for we are expecting You. You are very welcome, as we are hiding your latter-day purposes in our deepest hearts, joyfully losing our lives. Come, Lord, and destroy the walls of latter-day Jerichos that have withstood You in our day, and use us as your 'spies' and representatives of the Kingdom. As Rahab cried out in her day, we too proclaim in this hour: "the Lord He *is* God, the Lord *is* the One true living God!"

Thank You, Father, for sending us Your spirit of restoration, Your spirit of grace, to prepare us for the days ahead. We welcome and honor Him. Amen!

Chapter 8

Receive Your Mantle From Faith's Hall of Fame

As our ancestors of faith, let us also take our places in the present-day 'Hebrews 11 Hall of Fame/Faith.' May we too, one glorious day, find our own names among those listed in the halls of Heaven as the brave latter-day warriors who fought in the last great battle. May our names be among those who honored the King's commands to the very end, eagerly and joyfully pouring ourselves out for His purposes. May we run in the last great battle-marathon, living only to finish strong for His glory — no matter what the cost.

Let us each receive now from the Father's abundant heavenly storehouse our own present-day scripts and roles. Let us now take up those glorious anointings and mantles of destiny that will fulfill our heart's desires, carrying us into the fulfillment of our latter-day callings.

Let us walk as Enoch, in the mantle of pleasing God: *"And Enoch walked with God; and he was not, for God took him"* (Genesis 5:24). Enoch was taken up that he should not see death, for he obtained the witness that before being taken up, he was pleasing to God (see Hebrews 11:5).

As Abraham, let us receive the mantle of faith, causing us to look up and run to welcome God and His messengers of Good News (see Genesis 18). Let us believe that He who promised is faithful and able to perform His promise — no matter how long we have had to wait for it and no matter who or what we have had to leave behind. Let us, by faith, offer up our Isaacs, knowing that God is well able to provide a sacrifice for Himself. Let us receive His blessing, so that all the nations of the world will be blessed through us. And let us, even into our older age, receive our virility, enabling us to become spiritual fathers to multitudes.

Let us also, as Sarah, receive the mantle of faith, enabling us to conceive the child of promise, considering Him faithful who has promised. Let us, even into our older age, by faith, become 'fat' with the purposes of God, giving birth to the laughter of our Isaacs (see Genesis 21:6) and nursing our sons and daughters into their own destinies. As the Bride of Christ, may we be as glorious and beautiful in our advanced age as was Sarah (see Genesis 20), so that the kings of our day will also be drawn to us (or, rather, to the King whose glory shines through us).

Let us, as Rebekah, receive the mantle of drawing

Receive Your Mantle From Faith's Hall of Fame 125

water (see Genesis 24). Let us be found at the Lord's well, eagerly drawing rivers of living water for the tribes and tongues and peoples of the earth. Let us forsake all and respond quickly as the Holy Spirit fetches us and adorns us in preparation for our Isaac, our Bridegroom-Jesus. Let us longingly look for the Unnamed Servant and His camels who will take us on our journey to Jesus. Let us become intoxicated and lovesick with passion as we are drawn closer and closer to full union with our Bridegroom.

As Jacob, let us wrestle with the angel of the Lord all through our night of crisis. Let us wrestle 'til daybreak' and not let go until we obtain our blessing. As our morning of breakthrough dawns and we leave the battlefield with a limp, may we rejoice, as Israel, in our new name and new mantle of destiny.

As Joseph, may we receive the mantle of rulership, integrity and forgiveness. Let us hold fast to our dreams and visions as we are thrown into pits and sold into slavery by our jealous brothers. Let us remain forgiving and gracious as we serve in our own prison-houses, awaiting, in faith, our day of release. Let us remain steadfast and pure as we resist and flee from the many lustful advances of Potiphar's wife. May we joyfully offer refuge and restoration to our family and brothers in exchange for their jealousy and betrayal. May we rejoice greatly when the father and brothers that were lost are restored!

Let us, as Moses, receive the mantle of authority, bringing deliverance to entire nations through God's miraculous power. Let us choose to endure ill-treatment with the people of God, rather than enjoying the passing sinful pleasures of Pharaoh's palace. Let us consider the reproach of Christ greater riches than the treasures of Egypt, and let us look to the reward. Let us, by faith, leave our Egypts, enduring always by seeing Him who is unseen.

Let us lift high toward Heaven the staff of our faith, and let us stretch forth our hand boldly toward the Red Seas of our lives. Let us watch them part as the Holy Ghost comes blowing the fiery winds of our deliverance, providing a way of escape. Let us then turn around, as Moses did on the other side of the Red Sea, to yet again stretch out the same hand, with the same fiery double anointing, bringing forth a flood of destruction to every taskmaster and oppressive Egyptian-enemy in our lives.

Let us dance the dance of victory as Miriam, while enjoying the desperate sounds of the drowning Egyptian taskmasters who have bound and stolen from us and from our families for centuries.

Let us receive the mantle of leadership passed on from our forefathers, as Joshua received from Moses. Let us proclaim the challenge of our day, *"Choose you this day whom you will serve,"* and let us exhort our brethren as we proclaim, *"...as for me and my house, we will serve the Lord"* (Joshua 24:15, NKJ). May we, too, as Joshua, encounter God as the Captain of Armies and begin to march in rank with a holy vengeance. Let us march in faith and obedience seven times around our

Receive Your Mantle From Faith's Hall of Fame

last-day Jerichos, seeing them fall flat with the shout of victory. Let us seek God in every challenge and in every battle, receiving His divine strategies for victory. Let us be strong and courageous, taking the good land of God's promise before us, the land that is watered with *"the rain of heaven"*:

For the land, into which you are entering to possess it, is not like the land of Egypt from which you came, where you used to sow your seed and water it with your foot like a vegetable garden. But the land into which you are about to cross to possess it, a land of hills and valleys, drinks water from the rain of heaven, a land for which the LORD your God cares; the eyes of the LORD your God are always on it, from the beginning even to the end of the year.
And it shall come about, if you listen obediently to my commandments which I am commanding you today, to love the LORD your God and to serve Him with all your heart and all your soul, that He will give the rain for your land in its season, the early and late rain, that you may gather in your grain and your new wine and your oil. And He will give grass in your fields for your cattle, and you shall eat and be satisfied.
                                    Deuteronomy 11:10-15

As Gideon, let us receive the mantle to war valiantly against our present-day enemy-Midianites (see Judges 6-8). Let us first pull down and burn the idol-altars that are in our own lives, households and communities. Even if we have to do it at night and 'do it afraid,' let's just do it so that we will qualify for the Spirit of the Lord to anoint us, as He did Gideon, for the great battle ahead.

Let us rise up, forgetting that we are the least in our houses and of the least tribes (see Judges 6:15-16). Rather, let us become valiant warriors through God's mighty Spirit within. Let us not be sent home because of fear of the enemy, but let us receive and embrace our commissioning, destroy strongholds, join rank and go forward in the power of the Spirit to defeat the entire last-day enemy army. Let us go forth with the flaming torch of God's Spirit in one hand, while we sound the victory-blast on our shofars with the other. Let us watch as our confused enemy self-slaughters himself, and let us recover all that our enemies have stolen.

As David, may we receive the mantle of kingship, while inviting the Lord to live out His divine Kingship within us and through us. Let us receive the mantle of worship, as we offer songs of our God's faithfulness in our dark nights and caves, awaiting our day of deliverance. Let us show reverence for the Sauls in our lives, realizing that it is God who will destroy the old order. And let us throw off all religious constraints, as we dance with all our might, in spite of persecution and criticism, as we welcome home the precious ark of God's abiding presence (see 2 Samuel 6:14-23). Let us be known as a man or a woman after God's own heart. Let us give, as King David did, multiplied millions of dollars out of our own purses for the purpose of building God's Kingdom in this critical last day.

Receive Your Mantle From Faith's Hall of Fame 129

As Elijah, let us come out of obscurity to deliver the word of the Lord boldly to the kings of our day (see 1 Kings 17:1). Let us call down fire from Heaven upon the false gods and spiritual wickedness that rules in our day, allowing God to use us to draw a line in the sand, that the standards of righteousness and holiness would again be lifted high in our nation. Let us go up to the mountain of God to birth and welcome the rain that God has promised for our day. Let us receive the mantle of restoration, so that all things can be restored, preparing the way of our Lord's return (see Acts 3:21 and Matthew 17:11).

Let us, as the widow of Zarephath, receive our mantle of trust and complete surrender. Let us provide for the servants and purposes of God, even during times of hardship and drought, by giving all that we have — even down to our last meal. Let us welcome and house the prophetic anointing by our faith, sacrifice and obedience. Let us then receive back, in return, our dead, by the anointing we have nurtured and honored (see 1 Kings 17:8-24).

Let us team up, as Jehu, Elisha and Hazael, receiving the mantle of God's vengeance toward His enemies. May we, too, kill the entire house of Ahab and Jezebel, our spiritual enemies, pursuing them relentlessly until all their *"great men, ... acquaintances, and ... priests"* are destroyed (2 Kings 10:11). Let us go into their *"inner rooms"* and throw out their *"royal officers"* (2 Kings 10:25). Let us recall the word of the Lord to Elijah on the mountain, as he was sent forth to commission the three: *"...the one who escapes from the sword of Hazael, Jehu shall put to death, and the one who escapes from the sword of Jehu, Elisha shall put to death"* (1 Kings 19:17). Let us offer up ourselves as His 'battle-axes' and 'weapons of war.'

Let us rejoice with a holy vengeance, as the fire of our God goes before us, burning up His enemies (see Psalm 97:3). Let us celebrate as the powers of religion, idolatry, control and witchcraft that have bound the Church are broken and thrown down by this new double anointing and consumed by the fire of God's latter-day wrath.

Let us, as the Shunamite woman, receive the mantle of honoring the anointing. Let us have the good sense and spiritual discernment to recognize and receive the Lord's anointing and His anointed servants. May we, too, as the Shunamite, build 'upper rooms' in our hearts and lives to welcome and accommodate His anointing (see 2 Kings 4:9-10). Let us do whatever is necessary, joyfully expending ourselves and our resources, to provide lodging for the Father's great latter-day purposes. Let us furnish the upper chambers of our hearts with the godly character that would attract and draw His Spirit and His anointing, making Him feel welcome and pleased to dwell with us.

Let us, as the Shunamite, receive the mantle of a double-portion resurrection miracle. In response to tragedy, let us quickly carry our needs to the upper chamber-room of God's presence and lay them upon

Receive Your Mantle From Faith's Hall of Fame   131

the bed of faith, even as the Shunamite laid her dead son upon Elisha's bed, closing the door behind to all voices of fear and doubt. May we pursue, with great haste, the double-portion anointing of the prophetic spirit of Elijah/Elisha in this hour.

Even in our darkest hour, may we too answer as the Shunamite answered after her son died, *"it is well!"* Let us lay hold of the anointing, even as she laid hold of the prophet Elisha's feet: *"As the Lord lives and as you yourself live, I will not leave you"* (2 Kings 4:30). May we, in this hour, lay hold of the feet of the Anointed One, Jesus, and never, never let Him go. May we rejoice as we watch the double-portion resurrection spirit of Elijah/Elisha coming into our own households, resurrecting and restoring.

As Jehoshaphat, may we receive the mantle of prayer and fasting, as we are surrounded by our enemy-Moabites, Ammonites and Syrians (see 2 Chronicles 20). Let us also say to God in our battles, *"...nor do we know what to do, but our eyes are on Thee"* (2 Chronicles 20:12). Let us cry out from across this great land:

O Lord, the God of our fathers, art Thou not God in the heavens? And art Thou not ruler over all the kingdoms of the nations? Power and might are in Thy hand so that no one can stand against Thee.
2 Chronicles 20:6

Let us receive the word of the Lord from the prophet:

Do not fear or be dismayed because of this great multitude, for the battle is not yours but God's.
2 Chronicles 20:15

Let us trust in the Lord and in the words of His prophets:

You will not need to fight in this battle. Position yourselves, stand still and see the salvation of the Lord, who is with you, O Judah and Jerusalem!
2 Chronicles 20:17, NKJ

Let us, in this critical last-day, position ourselves in praise and worship, understanding that this last great battle is not ours, but the Lord's.

As we look at our own valley of dry bones, let us, as Ezekiel, receive the mantle of prophecy (see Ezekiel 37). As God asks us in our day, *"Son of man, can these bones live?"* Let us answer in faith, *"O Lord God, Thou knowest."* Let us prophesy under the unction of the great last-day anointing to the dead bones in our own lives and families, that they might not only live again, but that they would become *"an exceedingly great army."*

As Daniel, may we receive the mantle of wisdom and revelation, having favor with the kings of our day. Let us understand the times in which we live and, in heart-obedience, offer ourselves as living sacrifices. Let us open the window of our hearts toward Jerusalem to pray continually, and let us, being exiled to a heathen land or culture, not become defiled by the lifestyle of

Receive Your Mantle From Faith's Hall of Fame

the king or of those around us. Through wisdom from above, may we interpret the dreams of the leaders of our day, that they will declare, even as King Nebuchadnezzar, giving witness to the God of Daniel:

Surely your God is a God of gods and a Lord of kings and a revealer of mysteries, since you have been able to reveal this mystery. Daniel 2:47

Let us walk with God with such faith, integrity and passion that 'the lions of our day' will be compelled to shut their mouths in holy awe of the living God. Let us receive such favor from God that even the heathen kings will rejoice as they see us coming out of the lions' den unharmed. Upon finding Daniel unharmed, a second king, King Darius, also gave witness to Daniel's God:

I make a decree that in all the dominion of my kingdom men are to fear and tremble before the God of Daniel;

For He is the living God and enduring forever,
And His kingdom is one which will not be destroyed,
And His dominion will be forever.
He delivers and rescues and performs signs and wonders
In heaven and on earth,
Who has also delivered Daniel from the power of the lions. Daniel 6:26-27

Let us, as Daniel's fiery friends, Shadrach, Meshach, and Abednego, receive a mantle of courage and consecration toward our God. Let us rejoice as we are thrown into the holy fire so that all that is within us of man-pleasing, compromise and intimidation be burned up (see Daniel 3). Let us not fear the latter-day fire that is indeed 'seven-times hotter,' so that everything within us that would cause us to bow to false gods will be burned away.

Let us rejoice that there is the Fourth Man with us in the refiner's fire, enabling us to endure to the end. Let us rejoice in the moment that our King calls for us, bringing us out of the fire, knowing that all that has bound us has been burned up. Let us rejoice in knowing that the smell of smoke and the stink of compromise have been swallowed up in His fiery presence.

Let us take heart in knowing that He will not allow one of our hairs to be singed, nor will He allow the fire to destroy us. Let us rejoice that the kings of our day, as King Nebuchadnezzar, will glorify God as they see the Fourth Man in the fire with us (see Daniel 3:25), the one who looks both like a Lamb that was slain and like the victorious Lion of the Tribe of Judah. By our courage, faith and loyalty to Him in the fiery furnace of our afflictions, let us evoke the kings of our day to respond as King Nebuchadnezzar:

Blessed be the God of Shadrach, Meshach, and Abednego, who sent His angel and delivered His servants who trusted in Him, and they have frustrated

Receive Your Mantle From Faith's Hall of Fame 135

the king's word, and yielded their bodies, that they should not serve nor worship any god except their own God! ...there is no other God who can deliver like this. Daniel 3:28-29, NKJ

Let us team up, as Haggai the prophet, Zerubbabel the governor and Joshua the high priest, receiving the mantle of restoration to oversee the work of building God's house. Let us give ourselves to the work of restoration, for Heaven must retain Jesus until this period of restoration is completed (see Acts 3:21, Matthew 17:11 and Malachi 4:5).

When our moment of destiny arrives, let us receive the mantle of yielding and obeying, and say as Mary, *"Be it done unto me according to your word"* (Luke 1:38). Let us be so blessed with the impregnation of the divine seed of destiny that we are misunderstood, persecuted and pursued by the jealous religious kings of our day. Let us realize that there will be no room for us in the religious inns of acceptability, but let us be willing to birth our glorious destiny with the lowly and obscure in holy stables around the world, stables that are discovered only by angelic assistance.

Let us be willing, as Mary, to let a sword pierce our souls (see Luke 2:35), as we surrender everything for the nurture and fulfillment of His purpose. Let us be faithful, as we stand by, watching our own loved ones die on their crosses. Let us eagerly await resurrection morning, to see the stone rolled away, the tomb empty and the angels rejoicing. Let us not seek the living One among the dead, but let us find Him pouring forth His vibrant, eternal river of life into the highways and byways of our desperate, violent streets and cities. Let us become the mothers and fathers of destiny, not to be worshipped ourselves, but to love, nurture and protect the purposes of God in the earth today.

As Lazarus, Martha and Mary, let us receive the mantle of friendship with Jesus, always welcoming Him into our home. Let us choose the better part, as Mary, and sit at the feet of Jesus, worshipping and listening intently. As Martha, let us not be offended that Jesus purposely delayed in coming to our loved ones, arriving four days late and allowing them to die (see John 11), understanding that it was for the purpose of showing forth His glory in our resurrection.

Let us believe that He is able to resurrect that which is dead in our lives and families, and let us, in the power of His Spirit and Word, unwind and remove the graveclothes from one another. Let us come forth from the grave into His glorious life, liberty and joy. Let us show forth the works of the Son of God.

Let us, as Jesus, in our own gardens of Gethsemane, receive our mantle of complete surrender, saying, *"Not my will, but Thine be done."* Let us learn obedience by the things we suffer as we remain faithful and tireless through our 'silent years' of preparation. May we do and say only what the Father is doing and saying in this critical hour of preparation and harvest. May we watch and pray ceaselessly through the nights, that we may have the Bread of Life to break and give to many by day. May

Receive Your Mantle From Faith's Hall of Fame

we offer to all not only His salvation, but also healing, deliverance and miracles, the full abundant-life He purchased with His lifeblood.

May we not be offended as the Father turns away His gaze from us as we suffer unto death, unto the death of our fleshly self-lives. May we endure our own crosses and the weeping of the night for the joy that is set before us, knowing that our resurrection-morning is now at hand. May we be able to say at the end of our lives and service, *"It is finished"* (John 19:30).

On our journey as the good Samaritan, may we receive the mantle of mercy for the wounded and less-fortunate (see Luke 10:29-37). Let us seek for those who have been beaten, robbed and thrown into the ditches of religious forgetfulness. Let us offer our own oil and wine, our practical as well as our spiritual resources, to carry the wounded to a place of refuge, healing and restoration.

As Philip, may we receive the mantle of evangelism. Let us receive divine instructions from the angel, telling us where to go and which Ethiopian eunuchs to find. Let us 'preach Jesus' from the Scriptures and then baptize them in water. May the Spirit of the Lord snatch us away, as He translated Philip to another location to continue preaching the Gospel to all the cities (see Acts 8:39-40).

As the adulterous woman thrown at the feet of Jesus, may we receive the mantle of forgiveness and restoration (see John 8:1-12). Let us fall in love with the One who is gracious and kind to us, but also with the One who is stern before our accusers, vindicating us. Let us adore Him for His gentleness with us, for He understands us as no one else can. Let us rejoice as the Lord of the universe, the King of Glory, stoops down from His high and heavenly throne to join us in the sands of our lowly place of sin and shame, to love us and to lift us up yet again. Let us worship and adore Him as He forgives our sins and restores to us dignity and honor.

Let us, as Peter and John, receive the mantle of healing, proclaiming to the lame, *"In the name of Jesus Christ of Nazareth, rise up and walk"* (Acts 3:6, NKJ). Let us rejoice with those who are healed as they go walking and leaping and praising God.

When asked, as *Peter* on the day of Pentecost, *"What shall we do?"*, Let us be ready to answer as he did:

Repent, and let each of you be baptized in the name of Jesus Christ for the forgiveness of your sins; and you shall receive the gift of the Holy Spirit. For the promise is for you and your children, and for all who are far off, as many as the Lord our God shall call to Himself. Acts 2:37-39

Let us rejoice as we see three-thousand souls added to the Church in a single day.

As Peter, after denying and failing His Lord, let us return to feed His sheep with the mantle of mercy, restoring our fallen brethren (see Luke 22:32). Let us respond to our Lord's exhortation to love and tend His lambs. Let us go to the river at our Lord's bidding, to

Receive Your Mantle From Faith's Hall of Fame   139

catch that one fish that has our tax-money in his mouth. Let us not be surprised at our fiery trials, as though some strange thing were happening to us, but to the degree that we share in the sufferings of Christ, let us keep on rejoicing. As we suffer according to the will of God, let us entrust our souls to our faithful Creator in doing what is right.

As in Peter's later years of service, let us be willing to be taken where we don't want to go (see John 21:18). And let us take our second chance at not denying our Lord, to the point of being willing to be crucified upside down for His witness.

Let us, as Paul and Silas, after being beaten and thrown into jail for the sake of the Gospel, receive the mantle of worshiping Him through our midnight hours. Let us then be interrupted by 'a whole lot of shakin' as we are set free by a Holy Ghost earthquake. And in the aftermath, let us lead all those around us to the Lord (see Acts 16:25-34).

As Paul, let us receive the mantle of being poured out on the sacrifice and service of others' faith. Let us count whatever things were gain to us to be loss for the sake of Christ. May we come to know Him and the power of His resurrection, as we are willing to fellowship with His sufferings, being conformed to His death. May we forget all that lies behind, reaching forward to our glorious destiny ahead. Let us *"press on toward the goal for the prize of the upward call of God in Christ Jesus"* (Philippians 3:14).

As John the Beloved, may we receive the mantle of

intimacy with our Master, as we 'lay our head' continually upon His bosom (see John 13:23). Let us be among the disciples chosen to go with Him to the Mount of Transfiguration. Let us also be known as transmitters and apostles of love:

See how great a love the Father has bestowed upon us, that we should be called children of God; and such we are. ... Beloved, now we are children of God, and it has not appeared as yet what we shall be.
1 John 3:1-2

As we abide in Him, let us also walk as He Himself walked (see 1 John 2:6). Let us be willing to be persecuted and exiled to our own Islands of Patmos to receive visions of the end-time and to exhort our brethren.

As John the Baptist, may we receive the prophetic mantle of that heavenly voice crying in the wildernesses of our day, preaching a baptism of repentance for the forgiveness of sins: *"Repent, for the kingdom of heaven is at hand"* (Matthew 3:2). Let our voice be *"the ... one crying in the wilderness, 'Make ready the way of the Lord, make His paths straight' "* (Matthew 3:3).

Let us, as John:

...go before Him [Jesus] in the spirit and power of Elijah, 'to turn the hearts of the fathers to the children,' and the disobedient to the wisdom of the just, to make ready a people prepared for the Lord.
Luke 1:17, NKJ

Receive Your Mantle From Faith's Hall of Fame

Let us have the Holy Ghost courage to confront the spirit of harlotry in our day, even though it may cost us our heads, as we are made sport of by the king's party. Let us be willing to decrease, so that Jesus might increase. Let us bear witness of the True Light, that all through Him might believe. Let us be willing to live in consecrated and sanctified wildernesses of holiness, being different and unaccepted by the crowd.

And then there are the mantles of those who have passed this century. There was Papa Seymour of Azusa Street, Los Angeles, California, at the beginning of the century. There was the young Evan Roberts who spearheaded the Welsh revival, along with several other young people. What about the powerful mantles of A.A. Allen, Smith Wigglesworth, and John G. Lake, and the great women, Kathryn Kuhlman, Aimee Semple McPherson, and Marie Woodsworth-Etter? And time would not permit us to discuss in detail the mantles of generals who have passed more recently, like John Osteen, Lester Sumrall, and our beloved Ruth W. Heflin. Let us each now rise up and embrace our own personal mantle of glory!

Chapter 9

It's Our Turn Now

Let us now, as latter-day warriors, discover *our* roles, take *our* places and fulfill *our* destinies. Let us now throw off the graveclothes of earthiness and dullness and put on our new shimmering mantles of double-portion glory. Let us now be consumed with loving passion for the desires of our Father-Director, and let us act out our callings with a fiery determination.

We must persuade the multitudes upon multitudes of lost souls in the audience of this dying world that there is a living God who is good and whose name is Jesus. Let us reveal to them, through our Holy Ghost performance, that the God of Daniel is still able to deliver those who call on His name from the mouths of present-day lions. Let us show them the God of Elijah, so that all the Ahabs and peoples of the earth may have a chance to witness and worship the one true King and Lord who still answers by fire. When men behold Him as He is, they will cry out in holy awe, *"The Lord, He is God! The Lord, He is God!"* (1 Kings 18:39, NKJ).

The Concerned Father: "Search Out the Lost"

Let us not be distracted by the weights and cares of our own agendas and self-lives, but let us run with a holy vengeance and a tenacious endurance the fiery race that is set before us. Let us set our faces toward the Father and His latter-day purposes. As disciples of the Master Fisherman, let us come together in love and humility to prepare the glorious, massive end-time net.

Let us all take our places at the net, so that it can be cast over the whole earth at His bidding. Let us reveal the God of Noah, while multitudes upon multitudes of the audience of perishing souls are rescued and drawn out from the raging waters of deep darkness and last-day deception. Let us show them Jesus, the only Door of the Ark. Let us perform swiftly because the Ark-Door cannot remain open for long, for the curtain of the last act is soon to come down.

The latter-day rains have begun to fall, rains of mercy, deliverance and restoration. When Jesus stretched open His arms of love on Calvary, the Ark-Door was opened so that *'whosoever will'* could come in and be rescued.

> "Take My Father's heart of love for the dying, and go, and go swiftly," says the Lord. "Throw

out the lifelines of My hope and forgiveness, for I am the Shepherd who has left the ninety-nine to search out that one who is lost and perishing. Step forward with your shepherd's rod and staff, My people, indeed with your new mantles of double anointing, and search the ends of the earth for My perishing ones," pleads the concerned Father-Shepherd.

The Lamb Awaits

Let us not keep the King of Glory, the Lamb-Bridegroom, waiting, as He cannot return until the Bride prepares the way for His return;

Repent therefore and be converted, that your sins may be blotted out, so that times of refreshing may come from the presence of the Lord, and that He may send Jesus Christ, who was preached to you before, whom heaven must receive until the times of restoration of all things, which God has spoken by the mouth of all His holy prophets since the world began.
Acts 3:19-21, NKJ

Let us not disappoint the great cloud of witnesses who are beholding the greatest battle of all the ages. May they be overcome with the glory, splendor, and majesty of the Captain-of-Armies as He commands His troops in the victory of the Lamb and His glorious warrior-Bride in the culmination of the ages. Let us hear Him say of our latter-day performance on that glorious day, "Well done, good and faithful servant! Enter into the joy of your Lord!" Amen!

Part II

To the Women

Chapter 10

Jesus, the True Friend of Women

Jesus is, and always has been, the true Friend and Emancipator of women. When He walked and ministered among them long ago, He so kindly loved and honored them, always vindicating them before their condemning persecutors. In return, the women loved and followed Him, supporting and caring for His needs (see Luke 8:1-3).

This is the same Jesus who came aside to talk with the Samaritan woman at Jacob's well long ago (see John 4:5-30). His disciples, affected by the culture of the day, were perplexed, wondering why He was talking with a woman. As He spoke with this woman, not only were her past and present unveiled, but also her deepest heart. He revealed Himself to her as the Living Water that would quench her thirst forever, becoming in her a fountain of water springing up into everlasting life. This woman ran into the city, telling everyone about the Man that knew everything about her. Her life was changed forever through this one encounter with the Man named Jesus.

Jesus, who is *"the same yesterday, today, and forever,"* continues to lovingly approach all women everywhere in this critical last day. He is ever so gently drawing all to Himself, respecting and honoring us, desiring our friendship. Just as He did for the Samaritan woman, He is removing the shadows of our past, unveiling our deepest hearts and revealing to us our glorious destinies and futures. In the fierce and unrelenting last-day heat, He is offering to us rivers of His refreshing waters of life, so that we, too, might never thirst again.

Long ago, when the scribes and Pharisees sought to trick Jesus by bringing to Him the woman caught in adultery, He did not hesitate to defend her. They threw her at His feet and watched intently to see what His reaction would be. But rather than looking for a stone with which to punish her, Jesus kindly stood with her, ignoring her accusers, while drawing in the sand beside her.

The men continued questioning Him about the matter, until finally He stood up and vindicated the woman by addressing the sin of her accusers, causing them to leave. Only then did Jesus very lovingly admonish the woman, *"Neither do I condemn you; go and sin no more"* (John 8:11, NKJ).

"I Am Coming to You"

"I am coming to you today, My last-day women," promises your Father, "to lift you up, to restore

Jesus, the True Friend of Women

that which has been stolen from you, [1] and to avenge you before your enemies. [2] Even as the children of Israel long ago looked to Moses and then to Joshua for their deliverance, even so look to Me now, My daughters, for I am coming to you and to your households in this late hour."

Yes, our Lord is coming and revealing Himself to women today as their resurrected Lord, just as He came to Mary Magdalene the morning of His resurrection. Was it not the women who sought Him early that day, even while it was still dark (see John 20:1)? And when the others had come and gone, who tarried, looking into the tomb and weeping? Was it not His beloved Mary? He revealed Himself to her first that morning, and so is He now coming in the early morning of this new day to His faithful women.

Mary was not able to cling to Jesus and hold onto Him then, because He had not yet ascended to the Father. But today He is inviting us, as His daughters, to draw near and touch Him and behold His glory. But please, do not seek Him in the tombs of religion. As the angels have said, *"Why do you seek the living among the dead?"* (Luke 24:5, NKJ).

"I will come to you who have wept many tears at My cross, seeking Me through your long, dark nights of tribulation," promises your faithful Father. "But it is time now, My daughters, to behold the glory of your resurrection morning and the glory of your resurrected Lord!

"Yes, I am approaching and speaking to women in this hour," repeats the Lord. "Indeed, just as women stood by Me in My hour of humiliation and suffering on the cross, [3] so will I now stand by them in their hour of need. And who brought Me gifts, perfumes and spices at the tomb — was it not My beloved women? [4] And as you, My last-day daughters, have offered to Me your love-gifts of adoration and faithfulness in this challenging day, even so will I give to you My gifts — the spices and fragrances of My love and latter-day glory to repay and honor you," promises your Bridegroom.

A Woman Knew

Long ago, when Jesus visited in Bethany, very shortly before His crucifixion, it was a woman, Mary, the sister of Martha and Lazarus, who came to Him to prepare His body for burial (see Matthew 26:1-13). As Jesus had shared the imminence of the cross with His disciples, they simply did not understand, but a woman knew. Mary responded out of the depths of her love and intimacy with Him, knowing that His hour of suffering was at hand.

Jesus, the True Friend of Women

This was the same Mary who was chided once before for sitting at His feet, listening to Him teach, while her sister Martha was serving. Did He not tell her that she had chosen the better part, and that it would not be taken away from her (see Luke 10:39-42)? For as she sat at His precious feet, she came to know His deepest heart.

As Jesus visited the home of Simon the leper, none of His disciples gave Him water for the washing of His feet, but a woman wet His feet with her many tears of adoration and gently wiped them dry with her own hair. As He said to Simon that day:

> *You gave Me no kiss; but she, since the time I came in, has not ceased to kiss My feet. You did not anoint My head with oil, but she anointed My feet with perfume.*   Luke 7:45-46

The whole house was gloriously filled that day long ago with the lavishness and fragrance of this one woman's love and adoration for Jesus.

"Let Her Alone!"

Those who were around at Simon's house that day were scolding the woman because she had broken a very costly alabaster vial of perfume to anoint Him. They were indignant, thinking this had been a wasteful act. But Jesus defended her:

Let her alone; why do you bother her? She has done a good deed to Me .... She has done what she could; she has anointed My body beforehand for the burial.
Mark 14:6-8

"I am again coming to My women in this late hour," says the Lord, "to defend you before your persecutors. Yes, it is My women who have sought Me and anointed Me with many tears. You may not have known that your tears, My daughters, were washing and caressing My feet. And in the faithfulness of your love, looking toward your own crosses, you have lovingly kissed My feet," explains the Lord of glory.

"Yes, many of you have also been scolded and misunderstood by those around in your day, but I want you to know, My daughters, I have loved and received each and every tear that you have ever wept in My presence. Your adoration has welcomed and refreshed Me, even as the woman's did at Simon's house that day when I was looking toward the cruelty of Calvary. Know that I have not missed even one of your tears, and no, I am not ashamed of your weeping. Indeed, I am now saying again to all those around you in this last-day: *'Let her alone, why do you bother her, she has done a good deed to Me ... She has done what she could.'* Even as Mary anointed

Me beforehand for My burial, you, My faithful last-day women, are anointing Me in preparation of My imminent return," explains your Lord.

The Better Part

"I am now visiting many households with My presence and My latter-day purposes in this late hour," explains the Father.

God's faithful women are now welcoming Him, even as Mary did in her day, sitting at His feet and listening to Him, adoring and worshipping Him, anointing Him with the fragrances of their deepest hearts. His faithful women have thrown off the religious constraints and persecutions of those around, abandoning themselves unashamedly to Him, seeking for that better part, that one thing, as Mary.

"As you have not been ashamed of Me, My dear ones, neither will I be ashamed of you, but I will honor you before My Father," declares your Bridegroom-Lord. "I am telling you today, as I told Mary in her day, the better part, that one thing you have chosen — intimacy with Me — can never be taken away from you. You, My women, have sought for and touched My very heart.

"Indeed, just as Mary's extravagance filled the whole house with the fragrance of love for Me that day long ago, so have your prayers and adorations in this day been as *'golden bowls full of incense'* before My throne," says the Lord. [5]

Beautiful Latter-Day Flower Girls

We must know that the perfume and fragrance of our passion toward our Lord and His purposes are not in vain. Indeed, our lavish expressions of love toward Him are helping to prepare the way for His return. We are to Him as those in a wedding, who reach into their baskets and throw flowers along the way, creating a fragrant pathway for the bridal party to follow. Devoted daughters, we have been chosen to be His beautiful latter-day flower girls in the wedding of all the ages!

Have we not consecrated ourselves to Him yet again and again, inviting Him to cut the rose stems of our own fleshly self-lives, so that the fragrant petals of our hearts could be picked and strewn adoringly before the Lamb-Bridegroom? These roses were cut and plucked one by one from the good soil of our own hearts, dears, as we have lovingly surrendered all unto Him, our Bridegroom. These petals are now providing a sweet fragrance for the others in the bridal party to follow as they smell the aroma of His presence:

But thanks be to God who ... manifests through us the

Jesus, the True Friend of Women 157

sweet aroma of the knowledge of Him in every place. For we are a fragrance of Christ to God.
                                2 Corinthians 2:14-15

"My wholly surrendered flower girls, you have the honor of being among the first in the bridal party," commends your proud Father. "For you have yielded to the last-day anointing, the spirit of Elijah, which is transforming and adorning you for your Beloved. Keep coming, My dear ones, for the way of the Lord must continue to be prepared. For I see your every act of faith and kindness toward Me. I see every rose petal of your adoration, obedience and sacrifice that is offered to Me. Keep coming, My beautiful ones, keep coming."

Reap With Joyful Shouting

"I want you to know, My daughters," comforts your Father, "those many tears you have shed over your lost loved ones are My tears, and your heart of compassion for lost husbands, children and family is indeed My heart of compassion. It is My Shepherd's heart, My Father's heart, that aches for My children that have been scattered over the whole earth as sheep without a shepherd."

As prisoners of hope in a very dry and thirsty land, daughters, it was your many tears that watered and kept alive the seedlings of the Lord's latter-day purposes. The religious disciples and false shepherds might have chided and mocked you, but He has always honored and cherished every tear, and you will see great reward and return for each one of them:

> *Those who sow in tears shall reap with joyful shouting.*
> *He who goes to and fro weeping, carrying his bag of seed,*
> *Shall indeed come again with a shout of joy, bringing his sheaves with him.*   Psalms 126:5-6

Many Samuels

And what more can be said about the strength, courage and faith of God's women? Was it not Hannah who, so long ago, sought Him year after year with bitter tears, asking for children? And was she not rebuked by the priest, as he misunderstood the depths of her agony, thinking she was drunk at the altar? (see 1 Samuel 1).

While still barren, Hannah, in faith, offered to God her firstborn. The Lord richly rewarded her with a prophet named Samuel, who brought forth God's word again to His people. After Hannah weaned her son, she then brought him to the Temple as a very young boy to serve, and she sewed him little linen robes year by year and took them to him.

> "Did I not choose Hannah's broken heart and empty womb," asks the Lord, "to show forth My glory, raising up for Myself a faithful priest who

would do according to what was in My heart? Did I not reward her with three more sons and two daughters? Do I not repay My faithful women?

"Even as women in this hour consecrate themselves and their wombs to Me, I will again fill their bellies and their lives with latter-day Samuels," declares the Lord. "These young double-portion prophets will walk before Me in holiness, bringing forth My fiery word of restoration to this latter-day generation. Indeed, just as I filled Elizabeth's womb with John the Baptist, so will I now fill your wombs, My latter-day women, with the sons and daughters who will prophesy and prepare the way of My return!" [6]

Endnotes:

1. See Joel 2:18-32.
2. See Isaiah 61:2.
3. See John 19:25.
4. See Luke 24:1-10.
5. See Revelation 5:8.
6. See Joel 2:28.

"Many of my strongest and mightiest last-day warriors are women!" rejoices the proud Father.

Chapter 11

Fierce Warrior-Women

Moving on to the many other courageous women in faith's hall of fame, do you recall Deborah and Jael, Israel's two warrior-women? They initiated and won the battle against the Canaanites long ago (see Judges 4-5). A woman prophetess, Deborah, was raised up to be judge over Israel during a time of severe oppression. She prophesied to the commander of Israel's army, Barak, God's battle instructions and the promise of victory. Because he was afraid, Barak requested that Deborah ride with him into battle.

Then another brave warrior-woman, Jael, routed the enemy's leader, Sisera, as he tried to escape. She enticed him into her tent, hid him in a rug for his 'protection,' and then ran a tent peg through his temple. These two women were God's warriors, His one-two punch, and together they delivered Israel from its oppressors.

"I am now calling forth My latter-day Deborahs

and Jaels," says the Lord, "to sound My trumpets and prophesy deliverance over Zion in this day. Yes, you are My lovely and tender daughters who have carried and birthed children, but are you not now also among My strongest and mightiest latter-day warriors? You are now becoming My *'battle-ax[es]'* and *'weapons of war'* in this late hour. [1] Many of My strongest and most effective warriors are women," rejoices the proud Warrior-Father.

Fellow-daughters, are we not well able, as Jael, through Holy Ghost cunning and the power of His fiery Spirit and Word, to entice the enemy into tents of destruction? Did the Father not tell the serpent in the garden that the seed of the woman would bruise his head (see Genesis 3:15), just as Jael ran the tent peg through the head of the enemy's leader? We must know, fellow-daughters, in this late hour, our very heels will *"tread down the wicked, for they shall be as ashes under the soles of your feet"* (Malachi 4:3). For this is that day that the prophet Malachi saw; the day of Elijah, the day of fire, and the day of the restoration of all things (see Matthew 17:11).

Courageous Esther

And do you remember Israel's warrior, Esther, who was very beautiful? Following her uncle Mordecai's counsel, she saved her people from sure destruction,

Fierce Warrior-Women

risking her own life to do it. She had a warrior heart of courage and was rewarded as the enemy of her people, Haaman, was hung on the gallows that he had built for Mordecai, her uncle. Haaman's ten sons were also hung, destroyed, along with seventy-five thousand others who were enemies of Israel. The faith, courage and obedience of one woman was multiplied to bring deliverance to an entire nation.

> "As you serve Me in this critical hour," says your Father, "risking all, as Esther, I will cause the enemy's plans to backfire, so that he self-destructs upon the gallows of his own evil plan, as Haaman did. You must understand, My dears, there is much, much more at stake in this last day than your own welfare."

Some may not realize that the gentle bosoms that nurse babes are the very same bosoms that burn with a deep resolve and an unquenchable fire against the enemies of God. His warrior-women are as fierce as the she bears whose cubs are threatened. We must understand that our Commander-Father will use whomever He chooses to use in this last great battle. All that you have been through, women, is not in vain. You have been in battle-training, and your time of service is truly at hand.

A Friend to the Widows

Was it not a single mother, a widow woman of

Zarephath, whom God chose out of all the households of the land to serve the prophet Elijah during the drought (see 1 Kings 17:9-24)? Did the Lord not pass over all those in Israel to find this one woman with a warrior-heart of trust in Him and in His prophet's word? This dear woman saw God's miracle provision for her household, daily finding that He was adding oil and flour to her kneading bowl:

> *The bin of flour was not used up, nor did the jar of oil run dry, according to the word of the Lord which He spoke by Elijah.*   1 Kings 17:16, NKJ

Later, she was rewarded again for housing God's prophet by seeing her dead son raised up through the prophet's anointing.

A second widow woman, of the wives of the sons of the prophets, feared losing her two sons into slavery (see 2 Kings 4:1-7). She cried out to a second double-portion prophet named Elisha. When he asked her what she had in the house, she replied, "Nothing except a jar of oil." She obeyed the prophet by borrowing vessels, until there were no more empty vessels. She paid her debts by selling the oil, which the Lord supplied for her supernaturally. In this way, she was able to protect her sons and live from what was left.

> "Am I not able to provide also for those who cry out to Me in this day?" asks your faithful Father. "Do you not know that I am the Husband of

the widow and the Father of the orphan in these last days? Give to Me all that is in your hand, as these two widows did, and see if I will not show forth My glory on your behalf. Just as the little boy with the fishes and loaves gave Jesus all that he had, so will I today multiply that which you place into My hand," promises your Father.

A Wise Woman Accommodates the Anointing

Do you recall the prominent Shunammite woman who discerned the anointing upon Elisha (2 Kings 4:8-37)? She petitioned her husband to build an upper chamber for the man of God to lodge in as he passed by. As Elisha asked her what she needed in return, she was delivered from barrenness, bearing a son. Indeed, this woman most likely conceived the same moment she determined in her heart to accommodate and bless the prophet, thus inviting the Lord's mighty Spirit to take up residence within her, bringing new life.

When the Shunammite's son was grown and grew sick one day and died, his mother's warrior-heart again sought God's Spirit in the man of God, refusing the sting of death. In faith she laid her dead son upon the bed of Elisha, closing the door behind her, shutting out all voices of fear and doubt. She then traveled in haste to the prophet, answering not once but twice along the way, *"It is well,"* even while her son lay dead. This woman sowed a double-portion faith reply in order to reap a double-portion miracle.

She refused the servant's offer of help, knowing that the spirit of resurrection power was upon the prophet Elisha. She declared, as she caught his feet, *"As the Lord lives and as you yourself live, I will not leave you"* (2 Kings 4:30). Elisha then arose, coming to the dead boy and laying his own body and double-portion anointing upon him, not once, but twice. The mother's valiant warrior-faith was rewarded, even as was the widow's of Zarephath, by having her son raised up. She battled against the cruelest and most intimidating enemy of all — death itself — and overcame!

This wise woman understood that provision for her needs and the needs of her household were found only in the Lord and in His anointing. She received and honored the prophet, thereby partaking of the prophet's reward. Such faith and courage are what is needed for the women of today to overcome their many challenges.

"I Am Coming to Restore"

"My last-day women, even as I sent Elijah to the widow of Zarephath and Elisha to the widow woman and to the Shunammite woman, so am I now sending you My double-portion spirit of Elijah/Elisha to restore your households," says the Lord. [2]

"As you welcome the spirit of Elijah, the greater anointing, into your households today, as these women of old welcomed the prophets into their households, I will begin the work of restoration. As you give Me your all, trusting Me, see if I will not faithfully fill your kneading bowls with an abundance of flour and oil, and your lives with double-portion resurrection power," promises your faithful Father.

"My brave last-day daughters, you must pursue with haste, and with all your strength, the anointing I am beginning to pour out in this strategic hour. You must pursue it, just as the Shunammite woman pursued Elisha after the death of her son. Make no stops along the way, My dear ones, but focus singlemindedly on your one goal, pursuing Me and My double-portion anointing in this hour," exhorts your Father.

"Lay Hold of My Feet of Glory"

"Indeed, you must lay hold of My anointing in this hour," says the Lord, "just as this woman laid hold of Elisha's feet. Lay hold of My feet of glory, daughters of Zion, and rejoice as My Father makes His enemies a footstool beneath them. [3] It is time to lay hold of the feet of the Son of Man, the feet that are standing in the middle of the seven golden lampstands of the churches, the feet that are like *'burnished bronze, when it has been caused to glow in a furnace.'* [4]

"Lay hold of, My daughters, the meekest feet that have ever walked the earth, the feet that were first worshiped in a stable in Bethlehem, the small feet that played in the streets of Nazareth. Adore the faithful feet that served in a carpenter's shop, and the weary feet that walked the dusty streets of Galilee long ago with twelve men. Worship the lovely feet that are still bringing Good News to all men in this day.

"Embrace, My latter-day women, the scarred feet that have carried Calvary's shame. Embrace, in this hour, the strongest feet that have borne the sins of the whole world. Receive now heavenly virtue from the bloody feet that were pierced even for your sins, My daughters. You must lay hold of your forgiveness, deliverance and restoration, for I have many blessings to bestow upon you, and I have much for you to do."

Don't Let Go!

Fellow-daughters, we must refuse to let go of our Lord in this hour, just as the Shunammite woman refused to let go of Elisha's feet until he arose and came to her son. For as we lay hold of His feet of glory, He too will arise and will come to lay His presence upon that which is dead in our households, resurrecting and restoring.

"Prove Me now," says your Father, "and see if I

Fierce Warrior-Women

will not birth through you the double-portion miracles you have been seeking from Me, even for many years. Is this not the hour of your vindication and restoration, My warrior-daughters? Look up and see that, instead of your shame, you shall have double honor and a double portion in the land." [5]

Fill Your Lamps and Keep Watching!

As the Lord's beautiful flower girls and beloved warrior-women, we must keep looking up. We must keep watching, for the hour is very late, and our Bridegroom is preparing for His soon return.

We must remember the parable of the ten virgins. They took their lamps, and went out to meet their bridegroom at midnight (see Matthew 25:1-13). We must not be as the five foolish virgins, who had not prepared and had no oil, only to be left behind when the bridegroom came.

> "My last-day women, you must draw deeply and continuously from the oil of My Spirit and Word as the midnight hour approaches," exhorts your Beloved.

We must resist the spirit of slumber that is upon the land, prepare ourselves and our lamps for the Lord's imminent return. Dear ones, we must not be as the slothful virgins who were surprised by the shout of the bridegroom's arrival at midnight, only to find that they were unprepared and left behind.

Heaven's prophetic clock will soon be ticking the midnight hour, and we will be hearing that glorious and awesome shout announcing the return of the Bridegroom. Remember, He said:

Two women will be grinding at the mill; one will be taken, and one will be left. Therefore be on the alert, for you do not know which day your Lord is coming.
Matthew 24:41-42

"Prepare, My daughters," says the Lord. "Trim your lamps, and keep watching for your beloved Bridegroom. Know that He is sending to you lavish love-gifts of the perfume and spices of His latter-day glory. Be encouraged, knowing that the forerunner of the bridal party, the spirit of Elijah, has been sent ahead of the Bridegroom to prepare the way," comforts the Father. [6]

Endnotes:

1. Jeremiah 51:20, NKJ.
2. See Matthew 17:11, Malachi 4 and Acts 3:19-21.
3. See Psalm 110:1.
4. Revelation 1:15.
5. See Isaiah 61:7.
6. See Matthew 17:11 and Malachi 4:1-6.

Chapter 12

Birth Pangs, Daughters of Zion

As the prophet Micah said of these latter days:

*For pangs have seized you like a woman in labor.
Be in pain, and labor to bring forth, O daughter of Zion,
Like a woman in birth pangs.*   Micah 4:9-10, NKJ

As Paul declared to the Roman believers:

For we know that the whole creation groans and labors with birth pangs together until now. Not only that, but we also who have the firstfruits of the Spirit, even we ourselves groan within ourselves.

Romans 8:22-23, NKJ

Heavenly Birth Canals

Daughters, we must lay hold of our Lord in this

hour, even as we would lay hold of our bedpost during childbirth, pulling against it. The waves of glory He is now sending will ripple through us, manifesting as birth pangs, ebbing and flowing even as the waves of the ocean. We must know that as we hold onto Him ever so tightly, He is using us as a heavenly canal for the birthing of His latter-day purposes, and even for the preparation of His return.

Indeed, has it not always been the women who have been willing to carry the Lord's seeds of destiny, not only within their wombs, but within their deepest hearts? Did not Mary, the mother of Jesus, respond to her heavenly messenger, *"Be it done unto me according to Thy word"* (Luke 2:38), thus receiving His divine Seed? We must be willing, daughters of Zion, as Mary, to let a sword pierce our own hearts to carry and deliver His latter-day purposes.

What about the mother of Moses? Did she not birth the future of an entire nation, covering and nurturing her infant son, the anointed deliverer? This brave woman stood as an intercessor, placing her own life between that of her child and the Pharaoh she defied, as she hid her son for three months. The heart of one woman was entrusted with the future of God's people. And eighty years later, did she not eat of the bread that she had cast upon the waters, being delivered from Pharaoh with the rest of her nation, by the same son she had birthed and protected?

Searching for Midwives and Mothers

As daughters of Zion, we must understand that

Birth Pangs, Daughters of Zion

God's latter-day purposes are just now being birthed into the earth. He is searching for mothers and midwives to birth and hide His infant-purposes, just as Moses' mother hid her infant son from the wrath of Pharaoh.

> "As you birth and cover My infant latter-day purposes in the earth," says your Father, "I will also care for you. When Moses returned to deliver the nation of Israel, the woman who had birthed and protected him, his very own mother, was definitely not left behind."

What about the Hebrew midwives, Shiphrah and Puah, who defied Pharaoh's edict to kill all the Hebrew boys as they were being born, risking their lives in so doing (see Exodus 1:15-22)? Through the courage of these two midwives, many sons grew to manhood, becoming the mighty nation of Israel!

> "Was I not good to these faithful midwives, establishing them in their own families? Do I not honor those who honor Me?" asks the Lord.

> "Indeed, I am now calling forth many latter-day Shiphrahs and Puahs, who will have the courage and strength to birth and midwife My purposes. I am looking for women who will risk it all for the purpose of birthing and covering My seed. My women in this hour are 'doubling;'

consecrating to Me, not only their natural seed and wombs, but also receiving the divine seed of destiny into their spiritual wombs and hearts as well," explains the Father.

"These dear ones are willing to be stretched in order to birth and deliver My great latter-day purposes. I am looking for women who love Me enough to travail and labor in the Spirit, in order to see My many latter-day prophecies come to pass," says your loving Father.

Latter-Day Annas Pray

Daughters of Zion, do you remember Anna, the prophetess, who was married only seven years, spending the rest of her widowhood praying and fasting, never leaving the Temple (see Luke 2:36-38)? She prayed and fasted decade upon decade, until she was eighty-four years of age. And when Joseph and Mary brought forth the child Jesus into the Temple to dedicate Him, she immediately recognized Him to be the embodiment of her lifetime of prayers and fastings.

Women, you are now as latter-day Annas, also prophesying and interceding for the Lord's imminent return, never leaving that inner-heart temple of trust and intercession. You are giving thanks, exhorting all to look up for the redemption of Jerusalem in this last day. And you can be sure that, one day soon, you will see the

Birth Pangs, Daughters of Zion

arrival of the Bridegroom Jesus, just as Anna saw the arrival of the infant Jesus in her day.

It's Bigger Than You

Daughters of Zion, as we hold onto our Lord more and more tightly, the birth pangs will become stronger and stronger, allowing Him to send a greater weight of glory through us. As we press deeper and deeper into the realms of His glory, we are becoming more and more grounded and more able to receive greater and greater voltages of divine electricity and fire power. But as the waves of glory increase, so must the birth pangs increase, rippling through us yet stronger and stronger.

We must understand that *"our light affliction, which is but for a moment,"* is working out the accomplishment of His latter-day purposes. As we focus on the unseen, on our Lord, in the birth pangs of our affliction, rather than focusing on our temporal circumstances, we know that He is working not only in us, and for us, but also through us, *"a far more exceeding and eternal weight of glory"* (2 Corinthians 4:17, NKJ).

> "You must realize, My dear ones," says your Father, "that what is happening to you is much, much bigger than your own circumstances and much bigger than even your own pain, for there are billions of babies to be birthed into the Kingdom in a very short time!

"Will you love Me enough to continue to offer yourselves as living sacrifices, even as heavenly birth canals, My latter-day Marys and Elizabeths?" asks the Lord. "For I have sent My Spirit of intercession to help you in your weakness:

For we do not know what we should pray for as we ought, but the Spirit Himself makes intercession for us with groanings which cannot be uttered.
Romans 8:26, NKJ

"You must remember that I have been interceding since I ascended to the Father, [1] and I consider your intercessions also to be of the utmost importance in this critical hour," exhorts your High Priest-Intercessor.

Birthing Elijah

We must understand, daughters of Zion, that we are birthing the Lord's double-portion spirit of Elijah/Elisha, the spirit of restoration, into the earth. Just as John the Baptist was sent to prepare the way for Jesus' ministry long ago, so is the spirit of Elijah being sent to prepare the way for the Lord's return. The spirit of Elijah will restore all things before His return (see Matthew 17:11). Heaven must retain Jesus *"until the times of restoration of all things, which God has spoken by the mouth of all His holy prophets since the world began"* (Acts 3:21, NKJ).

Birth Pangs, Daughters of Zion

> "I am using you, daughters of Zion, to birth the spirit of repentance, refreshing, restoration and even the return of My Son Jesus," [2] explains the Father. "Your intercessions and groanings are calling forth My people Israel back to their land of promise in fulfillment of prophecy, and your prayers are stirring My Bride to prepare for her Bridegroom's soon return."

Daughters, we must understand that our intercessions are 'priming the pump,' drawing up the deep living waters, that river of life that flows from the throne (see Revelation 22:1). We must keep drawing, fellow-daughters, just as Rebekah of old drew water for Abraham's servant and for all ten of his camels. We must be strong in the Lord and in the power of His might. We must draw and draw and draw some more, for there are many souls who are dying of thirst in this latter-day heat.

We must be encouraged, daughters, for little did Rebekah know, that fateful day at the well long ago, that the one she offered to serve would take her, the very next day, to meet her bridegroom. We must know that our travails and serving are drawing us closer and closer to our Bridegroom in this late hour.

Elijah's Travails Bring Rain

Do you understand that the spirit of travail is falling upon us, fellow-daughters, as it fell upon Elijah on Mt. Carmel? Surely you have heard the Lord say, even as He said to Elijah in his day, that the rain is coming. He is now drawing us up to His holy mountain to squat and birth, even as Elijah did seven times (see 1 Kings 18:41-45). This is the hour of travail, as the great harvest is ripe and hanging in the balance. Are we not, indeed, the latter-day daughters of Zion laboring in childbirth that the prophet Micah saw so many, many years ago (see Micah 4)? For the Lord has always chosen to birth His treasures and His purposes through earthen vessels.

We are birthing more than *the rain*, dear mothers of Zion, we are birthing *the reign* of the King of Kings and the Lord of Lords!

We are beginning to gather together from around the earth, like an army of Marys and Elizabeths, exhorting and encouraging one another. We are taking turns, birthing and midwifing one another, as the Lord's waves and birth pangs of glory and destiny ripple through us, accomplishing and delivering His purposes. We must understand that it is time to begin pushing and bearing down in the Spirit, for the time of the end is very near.

Do Not Faint

"Take heart, My daughters," says your Father, "and do not faint in your labors. Be encouraged and know that the season of reaping has begun. Have I not said that *'weeping may endure for a night, but joy comes in the morning,'* [3] and are we not now in the very early morning of a new day?

"My daughters, I challenge you to begin to enter into My rest. I will do this work through you, through My Spirit of travail. And as each birth pang subsides, begin now to enter into My rest and joy. It is imperative that you be strengthened and refreshed in between the birth pangs," says the Lord. "In your periods of rest, begin to look around and see the budding signs of restoration throughout the land, and be encouraged, My daughters. Be deeply convinced that your affliction and labor for Me are indeed producing *'a far more exceeding and eternal weight of glory'* that is now beginning to encompass the whole earth," comforts your Father-Lord.

Focus on the Joy

"Just as your own husband, the father of your children, stands by you and holds your hand in childbirth, know that I am standing by you in these last hours of your delivery. Call out to Me and grasp Me tightly; receive and drink deeply of the virtue and strength of Calvary that ever flows through My hand into yours. Just as your earthly husbands coached you to 'focus' during your delivery, even now am I coaching you to do the same. As I, your Savior, hung on Calvary's cruel cross, I endured by focusing on the joy set before Me, the joy of seeing many sons and daughters brought to glory. My daughters of

Zion, begin now to focus on the joy that is set before you, the joy of your bringing many sons and daughters before the Father. Focus on the joy of embracing your Bridegroom. Focus on the joy of entering the heavenly Jerusalem," exhorts the Lord.

The angel Gabriel prophesied long ago to the priest Zacharias about the coming birth of his son John the Baptist: *"... you will have joy and gladness, and many will rejoice at his birth"* (Luke 1:14, NKJ). Even so, are we also seeing the Lord's joy birthed around the earth in this hour. Jesus told His disciples shortly before His crucifixion, *"You will be sorrowful, but your sorrow shall be turned into joy"* (John 16:20). He further explained to them, *"A woman, when she is in labor, has sorrow because her hour has come; but as soon as she has given birth to the child, she no longer remembers the anguish, for joy that a human being has been born into the world"* (John 16:21, NKJ).

The joy we are beginning to experience, fellow-daughters, is the same joy that the infant John the Baptist felt when he leaped in his mother's womb, sensing the arrival of His Lord in Mary's womb. We must understand that the 'Elijah-baby' is now leaping in the spiritual womb of His people because the Lord Jesus is very near — and very soon to return. He is truly standing at the door, knocking on the hearts of all in this late hour (see Revelation 3:20).

We will share in the joy that Heaven celebrates when

even one sinner repents (see Luke 15:7). And how much more will we celebrate the multitudes upon multitudes who will soon be born from above. We are also beginning to taste of the joy of the new wine that was saved for last, the new wine that the Father is now beginning to pour out in anticipation of the wedding of the ages.

"I Will Repay Double"

As we offer ourselves as living sacrifices for the Lord's last-day purposes and for the restoration of His Body, daughters of Zion, know that He will come to our households in return.

> "As you build My house, know most assuredly that I will build yours," comforts your faithful Father. "I see your travail on behalf of your families, and I hear your intercessions for the lost and dying. I will indeed honor those many women who are birthing and midwifing My latter-day purposes, losing their own lives to do it. Did I not say that:
>
> *" '...unless a grain of wheat falls into the ground and dies, it remains alone; but if it dies, it produces much grain. He who loves his life will lose it, and he who hates his life in this world will keep it for eternal life. If anyone serves Me, let him follow Me; and where I am, there My servant will be also. If anyone serves Me, him My Father will honor.'*
>
> John 12:24-26, NKJ

"Surely I will honor your labors of faith and love toward Me, My dearest latter-day daughters of Zion. I will show you My goodness and glory in this late hour, establishing all that concerns you and your own households today, just as I did for My two Hebrew midwives long ago. Instead of your shame, you will have double honor and a double portion in the land," [4] promises your Father.

Faithful Friends, Enter Into the Joy of Your Master

Do you recall, fellow-daughters, the Parable of the Talents (see Matthew 25:14-30)? A certain man was about to go on a journey, so he entrusted his possessions and talents to his servants. After a long time, the master returned to find that two of his servants had invested his money, but the third was afraid and hid it. The master praised the two servants who had multiplied his talents, but, sadly, the third servant was cast into outer darkness.

"You must understand," explains your Father, "that I have entrusted into your hearts and into your spiritual wombs My latter-day infant-purposes, even as this master entrusted his talents to his servants. When I, as the Master, return one day soon, I desire to find that you have carried, birthed and nurtured the precious divine seed that I entrusted to you. Will I find that it has been multiplied, growing into a great harvest of souls? On that great and final day, may I be able to say to you, My beloved daughters of Zion:

" 'Well done, good and faithful servant; you were faithful over a few things, I will make you ruler over many things. Enter into the joy of your Lord.'
Matthew 25:21, NKJ

"My dear ones, says the Bridegroom:

" 'You are My friends, if you do whatever I command you. No longer do I call you servants, for a servant does not know what his master is doing; but I have called you friends, for all things that I heard from My Father I have made known to you.' "
John 15:14-15

Endnotes:

1. See Hebrews 7:25.
2. See Acts 3:19-21.
3. Psalm 30:5, NKJ.
4. See Isaiah 61:7.
5. John 15:14-15, NKJ.

Part III

To the Men

"I am searching for real men in this hour as never before," says the Father. "I need men of valor and courage, men who will step forward into their destinies and never look back."

Chapter 13

It's Your Turn

This is your hour, men. This is your hour to come forth into all that your heavenly Father has created you to be and to do. This is the appointed time in which the Lord has chosen to favor His people, and He has chosen you to be His ambassadors of leadership, strength and honor.

It is no accident that you are living in this most awesome hour in human history, for each one of you has a unique and critical role to play in the last-day events that must soon take place.

It is time to wake up, warriors, and shake off the complacency and slumber of the past. This is a new day, one unlike any you have ever seen. God is preparing His choice vessels for the challenging and critical days ahead, so listen to your Commander-Father, and rise up to embrace your callings and destiny, last-day sons.

"I need real men in this hour, as never before in history," says the Father-Recruiter. "I need men of vision and of courage, men who will forsake all out of their love for Me.

"For I am now calling heads of families 'to the wall' to restore marriages, families, and communities," says the Lord, "building with the one hand and fighting with the other. You must listen closely to Me and take your places, as many changes are coming very quickly. I, and I alone, know the battle plan of victory in this strategic hour, so you must trust Me completely as your wise and caring Father-General."

Enemies Steal and Oppress

You must understand, warriors, that you are going through what Israel went through in the days of Gideon (see Judges 6:1-6). For years, Israel was forced into caves of defeat, working and sowing only to have the enemy, the Midianites, come and steal all they had worked for.

You, too, men, have sown, much as Israel did in her day, only to have it stolen again by last-day enemy-Midianites. Just as Israel was forced to retreat into dens and caves, so have many in this day been forced into dens of debt, disillusionment and even into dark caves of doubt and despair. But you must know that the Lord has always waited until the darkest hour to show forth the splendor and glory of His provision and rescue. And He has chosen you, men, to be His agents of last-day deliverance. You have both the great honor and the

It's Your Turn

sober responsibility of becoming His latter-day heroes of the faith.

The Lord Is With You, Mighty Man of Valor

In order to deliver Israel from its oppressors, God raised up a man by the name of Gideon. Gideon was threshing wheat one day in the winepress, in order to hide it from the Midianites, when the Angel of the Lord appeared, saying:

The Lord is with you, you mighty man of valor!
Go in this might of yours, and you shall save Israel
from the hand of the Midianites. Have I not sent you?
Judges 6:12 and 14, NKJ

Gideon answered Him:

O my Lord, how can I save Israel? Indeed my clan is the weakest in Manasseh, and I am the least in my father's house.   Verse 15, NKJ

And the Lord said to him:

Surely I will be with you, and you shall defeat the Midianites as one man.   Verse 16, NKJ

"I am coming again in this day, My men," says the Father, "to my many last-day Gideon-sons, challenging them to step forward into their destinies.

"I need many warrior-leaders," says the Father. "I need men who are weary of being in bondage, and weary of having their families and possessions plundered again and again. I need men who will be completely obedient to the voice of My commands in this hour, trusting Me to bring deliverance and restoration, not only to themselves individually, but also to their families, cities and countries. For many have been in bondage to debt, to lusts and to complacency, but I am coming in great power to avenge them in this appointed hour," promises the faithful Father.

"Yes, you've suffered many trials and tribulations, and, no, they are not yet over, but know, My men, I am coming to you in this hour to vindicate you before your enemies. I am sending My messenger-Spirit to you, just as I sent the angel to Gideon. He will give you specific instructions, a divine plan of attack that will succeed in accomplishing My last-day purposes. For I have many exciting and critical missions for you, My men. Have I not sent you?"

The Sound of War Is at Hand

"Know that I will be with you, just as surely as I was with Gideon in his day. I have much to accomplish in this strategic hour, therefore, I am

It's Your Turn

awakening My warriors. The sound of war is at hand, My sons. I am calling My men to battle," declares the Divine Recruiter. "This is a battle that has already been won on Calvary two thousand years ago. I need latter-day Gideons who are available and willing to obey My commands, standing in the place of sure victory that I have already purchased with My own lifeblood. I need men who will recognize and honor the Lion-Commander in this late hour.

"It matters not that you feel inadequate and ill-equipped as Gideon did, for the great task ahead. The truth is, My sons, that you are inadequate and ill-equipped in your own strength. However, the good news is that this battle cannot, and will not, be fought in your own strength. Rather it will be fought in My strength, indeed, in the power of My latter-day might," rejoices your Warrior-Father.

"As My Son sacrificed His life on Calvary and was raised up three days later, I gave to Him all dominion and authority. He is now imparting that authority to faithful servants in the form of *Mantles of Glory*. Receive now your Gideon-mantles, My last-day warriors. Even as I said to Gideon in his day, so am I saying to you today, 'Surely I will be with you, and you will defeat the enemies of your families, neighborhoods and country, as well as your own personal enemies. Know that I will be with you to do it,' " promises your Father.

"Just Do It"

The Lord came to Gideon yet again. He told him to tear down the altar of Baal and the other idol that his father had and replace them with an altar to the Lord (see Judges 6:25-26).

Men, your Father is coming to you with the same message He brought to Gideon — it is time to pull down the strongholds of the enemy in your own lives and families. These strongholds and idols have drained your strength and your manhood. Gideon could not have fulfilled his destiny and delivered Israel if he had failed to obey in this regard. Although Gideon had already received his mission assignment, the Spirit fell upon him only after he was obedient (see Judges 6:34):

So Gideon took ten men from among his servants and did as the Lord had said to him. But because he feared his father's household and the men of the city too much to do it by day, he did it by night.
Judges 6:27, NKJ

You must realize, men, that real heroes are not those who wait until they feel confident and courageous before they act. Real heroes are those who act in obedience regardless of how difficult it is, regardless of how they

It's Your Turn

feel, and regardless of who will approve. Even if you must do it under the cover of night and do it afraid — just do it. Just obey! And know that just as God protected Gideon, so will He protect you.

"Only One Name"

"Although you may not have altars of Baal and Asherah as Gideon did, My last-day sons," explains your Father, "many other idols have been erected in this dark day of deceit. As you welcome and yield to My Spirit, He will enlighten you as to what influences must be eradicated and burnt up upon My altars of repentance and holiness. As you come into agreement with Me in this final hour, following My lead, know that you will truly see My vengeance poured out upon your enemies.

"I am reminding Zion in this late hour that there is but one God, and only one name under Heaven by which men might be saved — the name of My Son, Jesus. I am truly a jealous God, and I will not share My glory with any other," declares your Father.

Chapter 14

Like Father, Like Son

Men, as you seek the Father with all your heart, know that He will be found by you. Even as adopted children have the desire to know their biological parents, so the Lord has placed deep into the hearts of all men everywhere the desire to know their heavenly Father. And as you come to know Him, you will come to know yourself, men, for you were created in His own image and likeness.

You were created to fellowship with Him and to reflect His glory, men. You were created to have dominion over His Kingdom, ruling as His humble, but strong representatives and leaders. He created you to be faithful husbands and fathers, protecting, honoring and serving your wives and children. He created you to walk and talk with Him intimately in the cool of the day.

"I created you, not only in My own likeness and image," says your Father, "but I also breathed

My very own life-breath into you. And, My sons, I desire to breathe into you once again in this last day, breathing into you new life, abundant life and life eternal. I desire to breathe into you an understanding of your true identity and destiny in this most strategic time in history.

"Indeed, sons, you must understand that you were born of My seed, and that My greatness has been deposited deep within you. Know that I am sending the warmth of My sunshine and the watering of My Spirit in this hour to cause those seeds to burst forth in resurrection power. There is no power on earth, nor above, nor below the earth, that can compare to the resurrection power that I have placed within you. My champions, you are men of destiny, men of great purpose," says your Father.

"Seek Me"

"Seek Me while I may be found, for when you find Me, My sons, you will find your true selves. You will begin to understand why you have been restless and frustrated, as you've not known the purpose for which you were born. As you set your gaze upon Me in this hour, you will become transformed in My presence. Even as I called My disciples Peter, James and John up to the mount of transfiguration in their day,[1] so am

Like Father, Like Son

I calling you up to fellowship with Me, and to behold My glory in this hour. The only way to find true fulfillment, success and joy is to find Me.

"Many have filled their lives with counterfeits, with forces and influences that have deadened their frustration and emptiness. But it is time now to wake up and rise up, shaking off the old, dark counterfeits, because the real thing is finally arriving. Yes, My mantles of greater power are just now being placed upon the shoulders of My faithful servants, as I am empowering them to accomplish My last-day plan. If you want to be true 'movers and shakers' in this last day, My sons, step forward. Let Me teach you the ways of success and victory, the very mysteries of My Kingdom:

Come to Me …. Take My yoke upon you and learn from Me, for I am gentle and lowly in heart.
Matthew 11:28-29, NKJ

The Way Up Is Down

As you yield yourselves to the Father and His plans, just watch what He will do for you and through you. Many of you have tried to build your own kingdoms, following your own way, causing failure, discouragement and even disillusionment. You must die to your self-lives and self-ambitions, men, for there is only one pathway to true life and success. Yes, it is true that Jesus died on the cross of Calvary for you, but has He not said that you, too, must deny yourself, take up your own cross and follow Him (see Mark 8:34)? He went further:

> *For whoever desires to save his life will lose it, but whoever loses his life for My sake and the gospel's will save it.*   Mark 8:35, NKJ

Understand that the Lord cannot and will not place His great latter-day mantles of glory and power upon self-willed and ambitious men. You must die before you can live, and you must submit to His Fatherhood and authority before you can represent Him before others. You must understand the great mystery of His Kingdom — the way up is down.

You must offer yourselves to God daily as living sacrifices, following Jesus' example. When He walked the earth, He did not live by His own desires, but He sought the Father continually, doing and saying only what the Father was doing and saying (see John 5:19). Jesus' prayers were always answered because He prayed according to the Father's will, because His heart was one with Him, and His only desire was to please and glorify His Father.

"Follow Jesus' example of obedience and intimacy with Me, My sons, and you will find not only life-eternal, but also victory and fruitfulness in every area of your lives," promises your Father.

Discover Your Mantle!

As you come to Him, last-day warriors, abiding in the cool, deep, and clear waters of His presence, He will begin to satisfy your heart's longings and desires. You will be very deeply refreshed and satisfied, and you will be strengthened and encouraged. You will begin to understand about the day in which you live and about your specific role in it. You will become clearer and clearer in regard to your latter-day missions, understanding what your gifts and callings are, discovering just which of the *Mantles of Glory* you have been destined to wear from the very beginning.

God has designed and prepared many unique and diverse mantles, or anointings, for His men in this late hour. In His infinite creativity, know that no two of them will be the same. Your mantles of anointings will be as individual as you are, men. Many of you have had dreams and visions that the Lord placed within you from long ago. Others of you will just now be receiving, or becoming aware of, your dreams and heart's desires. The Lord is now beginning to send forth the mantles of anointing that will empower and enable you to fulfill those desires and dreams.

It is time to step forward, men, for God is beginning to remove the veil from many, revealing their true identity, talents and giftings. He has hidden and reserved you, just as a wise, mighty captain who conceals his choice weapons until just the right moment. Latter-day champions, you have no idea what is just ahead. The thrills and fun are just beginning!

"You have looked for fulfillment and satisfaction in many arenas, My sons," explains your Father, "but know that you will find it only in intimacy with Me and My latter-day plans. This is what I created you for, and it is the only thing that will satisfy you. Know that I custom-created and custom-designed you for the purpose of fulfilling My last-day plans.

"My sons, you are like the finest quality of race cars. For so long you have been forced to drive upon the streets of mediocrity, confined and restrained, but now you must know that the day of your deliverance is at hand. As you seek Me in this hour, know that I am bringing you into a new place of release, to a place where you can 'floor it' and begin to express all that I have put within you. Many of My sons are returning home to Me in this final hour, finding their places on the starting line of destiny's racetrack, revving their engines and waiting. But the time of waiting is very quickly coming to an end, men, so get ready. The hour for which you were created is truly at hand," encourages your Father.

Like Father, Like Son

Needed: More Than "A Few Good Men"

Awake, men, for this is your appointed hour of restoration. The Lord is coming to restore your honor, warriors. This is truly the great battle of all the ages, and the divine Commander-in-Chief is challenging you to enlist in His service.

There are only two sides in this great battle — good and evil, light and darkness, His truth and the enemy's deceit. Do not be deceived into thinking there are gray areas between the two, for the only gray area between the two is a great, eternal chasm that has been fixed, a time-space gap that separates Heaven and Hell forever (see Luke 16:26). Men, this is not just another video-movie fantasy. This is truly the showdown of all the ages. And your decisions will determine how you, and others around you, spend eternity.

It is time now to go into battle for your families, for your neighborhoods and cities, and even for your country. *"For such a time as this"* have you been created, men. God is now calling forth His dreaded latter-day champions of the faith, drafting you by His Holy Spirit.

> "I am going into your homes and into your hearts," announces your Father-Recruiter, "throwing off the blankets and covers of slumber and complacency. I am awakening you to your latter-day anointings, the mantles of destiny, which you were born to bear. This is it, men! Hear My Holy Ghost bugle resounding

from city to city, from sea to shining sea! We are in the very early morning hours of a new day, the day of restoration, the day of Elijah. ²My angels are sounding the wake-up alarm, My prophets are prophesying deliverance from the east to the west, and My people are blowing their victory shofars from Mount Zion!

"It is time to start training My sons, as the greatest army of all time is indeed needing more than 'a few good men.' It is time to hit the floor, doing Holy Ghost push-ups and sit-ups, toning up those sagging spiritual muscles that have grown stiff and weak during your long season of slumber and ease. Come forth, My warriors, come forth in the power of My latter-day might," exhorts the great Warrior-Father.

A Kingly Lion to Command Mighty Men

Be assured, warriors, that the Lamb that willingly laid down His life on Calvary's cross two thousand years ago is now returning as the kingly Lion. He is reclaiming His territory and His Bride, commanding His warrior-troops in the last battle. Will you march with Him into the great battle, champions? Which of you will go down in the annals of Heaven as His noble latter-day mighty men? Who of you will display extraordinary feats of faith and courage, doing great exploits in His name? Who of you will follow Him into the highways

Like Father, Like Son

and byways of lost humanity in this hour of deep darkness? And who will run with the torch of His Good News and mercy, bringing life everlasting to all who will receive it?

> "It is time to shake off the doldrums and mediocrity of the past," says your Father, "for I am breathing new life into you in this critical hour. I am just beginning to pour out a very great anointing of power that will enable you to fulfill your destinies, My sons. I am just beginning to pass out spiritual weaponry that has been reserved for this last-day battle. Indeed, I am passing out anointings that will begin to accomplish the greater works that Jesus prophesied for the last days. The anointings and spiritual weaponry that I am beginning to pour out are unprecedented, for they will be even greater than that which I poured out long ago upon My servant Moses in order to break the power of Pharaoh over My people."

Your Rescue-Mission: Many POW's

Men, there are multitudes upon multitudes in the valleys of decision in this late hour (see Joel 3:14)! There are multitudes of spiritual prisoners of war that have been overcome by the deep darkness that is now upon the face of the earth (see Isaiah 60:2). The caring Father is calling forth His dreaded last-day warriors who will move in great courage and wisdom, blasting open prison doors with His explosive resurrection-power. He will send forth His mantle of greater anointing upon them, enabling them to *"proclaim liberty to the captives, and the opening of the prison to those who are bound"* (Isaiah 61:1, NKJ).

This is your mission, men, to set the captives free. Even as the children of Israel were not free to serve and worship God while they were under the oppression of the pharaoh of Egypt long ago, so in this last day are there many who are bound and oppressed by darkness and deception. Go with the rod of God's authority, men, and break the power of the enemy, that these might be free to serve and worship the Lord in spirit and in truth.

"This is indeed the appointed hour of rescue for My people," explains the Father. "This is the day that My prophet Malachi saw from afar when he said, *'You shall trample the wicked, for they shall be ashes under the soles of your feet.'* [3] It is time to go into the camp of the enemy and reclaim what is rightfully Mine, My sons. As you take the title deed of Calvary with you, know that no force can withstand you."

"Go as My representatives, lifting high the Name above every name, and watch the prison doors fly open before you. Remember that two thousand years ago I disarmed principalities and powers, making a public spectacle of them, triumphing over them. [4] Know that I am giving you, My last-day sons, the mantle of double anointing and wisdom that will unlock even the very deepest and darkest of prisons. Multitudes of desperate POW's are waiting, and many are dying. It is time to rise up and prepare for battle, My great ones," challenges your Father.

Endnotes:

1. See Matthew 17:1-5.
2. See Matthew 17:11 and Malachi 4:5.
3. Malachi 4:3, NKJ.
4. See Colossians 2:15.

Chapter 15

Time to Press

The Holy Ghost will become your unrelenting Personal Trainer, men, forming and shaping you into the new man that the Father has destined you to be. Work with your Trainer, following His every suggestion, for He alone knows both your strengths and your weaknesses. He alone knows just what exercises and challenges you need to overcome and master to be prepared for victory. Please do not cast Him aside in this most critical hour, for in so doing, you may cast aside your very own destiny.

As you become weary from your labors, know that your Holy Ghost Trainer will be there to wipe your brow, and to give you a drink of living water, imparting renewed strength and vision to you. He will indeed be the toughest trainer you have ever met! But you can be assured that He will also care more for your eternal soul than anyone you've ever encountered.

There is much at stake, men. It is time to begin exercising your spiritual disciplines. It is time to become ruled by God's Spirit, rather than by your appetites:

For if you live according to the flesh you will die; but if by the Spirit you put to death the deeds of the body, you will live. For as many as are led by the Spirit of God, these are the sons of God.

Romans 8:13-14, NKJ

It is time to crucify your flesh, bringing its desires and lusts under the subjection of your Personal Trainer. He will know just what to do. He will teach you how to offer yourself as a living sacrifice again and again (see Romans 12:1). He will send you off on your exercise bike of faith, and He will keep you on the treadmill of endurance, for we are in marathon training, men. It is time to focus on your one goal — hearing and obeying His orders.

It is time to press, men, and press and press and press again, for this is the only way to victory. With all your might, you must *"press toward the goal for the prize of the upward call of God in Christ Jesus"* (Philippians 3:14, NKJ).

It is time to press into God, men, as a man named Zaccheus who lived long ago. He pressed through the crowd, climbing up into the sycamore tree to see Jesus. Little did Zaccheus know that Jesus would reward him with a personal visit in his home. As a result of Zaccheus' pressing in to see Jesus that day, salvation came to his house and changed his life forever.

Time to Press

> "And as you press into Me, My last-day champions, know that I will be waiting for you," promises your Father. "Know that I will be waiting to reveal Myself and My purposes to you in a very personal way, just as I did to Zaccheus. But you must know that you will have to press through crowds of the religious who have obscured My true identity in this hour. You may also have to press past the masses who have become lukewarm and complacent, those who are annoyed with your passion and zeal for Me. And just as Zaccheus climbed up into the sycamore tree to see Me, you too may have to climb above the opinions and approval of others as you seek to get a better look at who I really am."

You must press into God, men, as the disciple John who laid his head upon Jesus' bosom the night of the last supper (see John 13:23). It is imperative that you draw nearer and nearer as that awesome midnight hour approaches. He desires to reveal Himself intimately, imparting not only your destiny, but also His very own heart, nature and character into you. As you draw nearer to Him, and you allow Him to become intimate with you, He will set your very soul on fire, men.

> "As you fellowship with Me as the Consuming Fire that I am," explains your Father, "you, too, will begin to burn with an unquenchable fire,

consumed with My last-day passions for the lost and the dying and for My beloved Zion."

Last-Day Peters Will Be Restored

Press into Him, men, as the disciple Peter did that fateful morning. Recognizing the resurrected Lord standing on the shore and unwilling to wait for the others, he leapt off his fishing boat and started swimming (see John 21). That beautiful morning, Peter leapt into the waters of complete forgiveness and restoration. The unbearable yoke of guilt and shame caused by his triple denial of the Master was broken off, as he professed his love for Jesus, not once or twice, but three times. As Peter pressed into Him that day, he came to understand the power of His redemption, as well as the limitless depth of His forgiveness and love. Jesus exhorted Peter in regard to his callings, telling him to feed His lambs and tend His sheep, as well as speaking to him personally of his future.

> "My sons, as you press into Me in this last day," says your Father, "I will remove the heavy weights of guilt and shame that have been layered upon you for so long. As you leap off your comfort-boats of familiarity and bondage into My merciful waters, you, too, will find limitless depths of love, cleansing and redemption. I will speak to you of your giftings and callings and of

the work which you are to do as you follow Me. Full restoration is at hand, My last-day Peters.

"Some of you have thought that all was lost. But know that I am not only the God of the second chance, but rather I am the God of the seventieth chance. Many that served Me in the past have been broken and deeply disheartened, and some have almost fallen away. But know, My valiant Peters, I am pouring out a power and a love that will bring complete restoration in your life, and in your families and in your life's purpose.

"After his denial of Me, because of his shame, Peter had gone back to what was familiar to him — fishing — and also because he did not understand My kingdom purposes. But know, men, that the greater anointing I am beginning to pour out will forever annihilate your past and your shame. And I am now speaking to you about your futures, and what I have for you to do. You must look forward, My sons. Look forward into your glorious destinies that I have planned for you from long ago," exhorts your Father.

And do you remember Nicodemus, a ruler of the Jews long ago, who pressed into the Lord secretly by night, desiring to know the ways of the Kingdom (see John 3:1-21)? And while his fellow teachers were asleep, was he not richly rewarded, not only receiving a great wealth of truth, but also having a personal encounter with the Messiah Himself? Indeed, didn't this teacher of Israel come to understand that Yeshua the Messiah *was* the living Truth, the complete embodiment of all that he had studied and pursued? As he pressed into Jesus secretly that one night, was he not eternally rewarded, discovering the living Doorway into the Kingdom through being born from above (see John 1:12-13)?

> "My sons, it is time to press into the cloud of My latter-day glory. Do you recall how the Apostle Paul spoke of a man who was *'caught up into the third heaven,'* and *'into Paradise,'* hearing words that were *'inexpressible'*? [1] There are realms of My glory that you have not known, and I desire for you to experience them. You must allow the waves of glory to wash over you again and again, transforming you into the new man that I have destined you to be from the beginning of time. Please do not shy away from My manifest presence. Yes, it may be unfamiliar to you, but in it you will find everything you've been longing for. Press into Me, My sons, for I, your eternal Father, am eagerly waiting for you."

Restored Vision

You must press into Him, men, as blind Bartimaeus,

Time to Press

who heard that Jesus was passing by long ago and cried out. Those around tried to quiet him that day, but he only cried out all the more loudly, *"Son of David, have mercy on me!"* (Mark 10:46, NKJ). As Bartimaeus pressed into the Lord with all his might, Jesus responded by saying, *"Go your way; your faith has made you well"* (Mark 10:52, NKJ), and he was rewarded with the gift of his sight. And did Bartimaeus not receive a double blessing as he opened his eyes for the very first time? He did not see just anyone, but rather the Messiah Himself, therefore receiving not only physical eyesight, but spiritual vision and insight as well.

Know, men, that in this final hour the Lord is again passing by, and be assured that He hears your cries. Just as Bartimaeus would not be quieted, you, too, need to keep calling out with all your might, for He is coming. Your Messiah, the Lord of glory, is again walking the streets, the highways and the byways, searching for His chosen in this late hour.

> "And as you cry out to Me with all your might, as Bartimaeus did," says the Father, "I will begin to restore your eyesight, especially your spiritual eyesight and vision, My last-day champions of the faith. Many of you have been confused and discouraged because you have had no vision, no understanding of the day in which you live, nor of your role in it. I am restoring vision and the gifts of revelation in this strategic hour, My sons.

"What kind of general would allow his soldiers to go into battle with dim eyesight, or none at all?" asks your caring Father. "Indeed, many of My sons do not even know that the greatest battle of all the ages is at hand because they cannot see past their own temporal circumstances. This must change — and very soon! Allow Me to touch your hearts, My sons, so that *'the eyes of your understanding [will be] enlightened; that you may know what is the hope of His calling.'* [2]

"As you come to Me and abide in Me, I will begin to give you Heaven's perspective, so that you can see through My eyes the unfolding battle that is upon us. I will be giving to you all the 'divine intelligence' information that you will have need of to accomplish My purposes and bring about victory. And as I restore your spiritual sight, you will begin to see Me as I truly am," says your Father.

Even though Bartimaeus may have heard about the coming Messiah through the teaching of the Scriptures, his sight could not be restored completely until he had a personal encounter with the Messiah Himself. When his eyes were opened for the first time, he saw his Healer, Savior, Deliverer and Provider — his All-in-All. All the bounties of Heaven filled his vision and his focus that sovereign day.

"As you continue to focus on Me, My sons," says your Father, "I will not only fill your vision, I will become your vision. As I develop your spiritual eyesight, you will behold Me in My glory. You will begin to comprehend with the eyes of your spirit who I really am, not who others have told you that I am, but who I really am. You must see and know Me for yourself in this late hour."

A New Backbone

The Lord is placing a spiritual backbone into you, men, so that you will be able to stand against the wiles of the enemy in this evil day. He is imparting His Word into you, line upon line, precept upon precept, forming an eternal backbone that will be able to bear the weight of latter-day glory that He is sending forth in great measure in this day. This Word is His life-breath and is proceeding from His mouth even now.

Just as He created all things by the breath of His mouth in the beginning, so is He again doing a creative thing in the earth, as He speaks and prophesies eternal substance into you. Are you not feeling a sense of strength coming into your inward parts? Are you not, indeed, beginning to rise up, standing straighter and taller? Are you not beginning to feel the yokes of bondage loosening and even falling off, as the Lord turns up the heat of His anointing in this final hour? Even as He spoke long ago to Israel:

I am the Lord your God who brought you out of the land of Egypt, that you should not be their slaves; I have broken the bands of your yoke and made you walk upright.   Leviticus 26:13

The Father Recruits Real Men

"I need brave men of action and adventure who will be the cast of players in the last great battle-drama," says the Father. "I need men who know the heart of their King and Father, reflecting not only His strength, but also His mercy and lovingkindness. I need vessels of perfect love, those who will become channels of the greater works. I need vessels who will reflect the character of the Lamb as well as the kingship of the Lion.

"I need men who have fire shut up in their bones. I need men who are consumed with zeal for My house and for My last-day purposes. I need men who are not afraid to lose themselves to the deep, powerful, and glorious currents of My river. I need men who are not afraid of being weak in themselves, but strong in Me. I need men who will trust Me completely to draw them into the heart of My will, being assured that they will fulfill their highest destiny," calls the Recruiter-Father.

The Spirit and the Word Married

Know, men, that this great last-day revival will be characterized by the marriage of God's Holy Spirit and His Word. The emphasis will not be on one or the other, for the two will be working together for the accomplishing of His last-day purposes. For how could Jesus, who is the living Word incarnate, be separated from the third Person of the Trinity, the precious Holy Spirit? *"And the Word became flesh and dwelt among us, and we beheld His glory, the glory as of the only begotten of the Father, full of grace and truth"* (John 1:14, NKJ).

Are not the Father, Son and Holy Spirit Three in One and One in Three? In the beginning, God created the heavens and the earth by the words that He spoke, and He fashioned Adam out of the dust of the earth. But it was not until He bent over and breathed into man that he came to life and became a living being (see Genesis 2:7). It has always been God's Spirit and His Word together that bring life.

The same truth was revealed to the prophet Ezekiel, as he was caught up in the Spirit to a valley full of dry bones (see Ezekiel 37). As he prophesied the Word of the Lord, God connected them, bone to bone, put sinew onto them, and then skin, but they were still dead. It was not until His life-breath Spirit came into them that they came to life. His Word and His Spirit together created an exceedingly great army, and so will it be in this last day, beloved Zion.

"My children, do not displease Me by honoring My Spirit *or* My Word. You must honor *both* in order to be who you are called to be and to do what you are called to do," explains the Father. "The two are, and always have been, inseparably married to one another and to My will. Those who walk according to My heart in these last days will step in cadence to My will, one step in My Word and the next in My Spirit. And you will discover that the two flow in and out of each other, the Spirit always pointing to Jesus, the living Word. But did Jesus not also testify of the Spirit that empowered Him to do the works and the will of the Father: *'The Spirit of the Lord is upon Me, because He has anointed Me'*?" [3]

Restored Manhood

Men, just as the men of Israel in Gideon's day had to deal with their enemies, the Midianites and Amalekites, so have you had to deal with enemy forces that have sought to destroy your manhood. Men, God, your Father, has had enough! He is now ready to destroy these spiritual forces of wickedness at their root (see Malachi 4:1). Just as He dealt long ago with King Ahab and his wife Jezebel and all her family, acquaintances, and royal officers, until they were utterly destroyed, so He is bringing about great deliverance in this hour.

"I created you from the beginning to be men — real men, strong men — like your Father-Creator. I am coming with great vengeance to destroy the forces that seek to confuse you, leaving you weak and compromised. Yes, My heart of lovingkindness and mercy is ever poured out toward all those who have been affected by these forces. But you must understand, My warriors, who the enemy is. You must understand that you do not wrestle against flesh and blood, but against principalities and powers of darkness that seek your destruction, [4] desiring to steal your manhood, strength and anointing," explains your Father.

"You have suffered much frustration and humiliation in this generation, My men, but know that your hour of vindication is at hand. Know that the forces of wickedness that have disdained your manhood and leadership are the very same forces that oppose My Fatherhood and authority. Indeed, these evil forces hate you because you are the representatives of My authority in the earth, just as I gave dominion to My son Adam in the garden so long ago. But know that the days of your enemies are numbered.

"I created you to be vessels of honor, My sons, reflecting My Fatherhood, strength and character, the very things that the enemy has sought so very desperately to destroy in you. But know that he will not succeed in his evil plan, for the Sun of Righteousness is now arising to those who fear His name. [5]

"As you receive and honor Me as your Father, My men, I will restore to you your manhood and dignity. And be assured, My courageous last-day warriors, I am for you, I am with you and I will accomplish through you My critical plans and purposes. I am with you to do it," promises your faithful Father. "Arise, sons, and take up your warrior mantles!"

Endnotes:

1. 2 Corinthians 12:2 and 4, NKJ.
2. Ephesians 1:18, NKJ.
3. Luke 4:18, NKJ.
4. See Ephesians 6:12.
5. See Malachi 4:2.

Part IV

To America

Chapter 16

My Beloved America

"Wake up, America! This is your hour, for your Deliverer has come," announces your Father-Founder. "Just as I came to Moses through the burning bush, so am I now coming to you to transform you and commission you to deliver the nations. Have I not saved you, America, for such a time as this? Was it not My Spirit of destiny and grace that led to the discovering and founding of this great nation so long ago? My Spirit of courage and divine purpose has been interwoven into the very foundation of this country from the very beginning. Did not the hearts of the founding fathers burn with passion from above for the future of this great new land?"

Your Greatest Hour

"Yes, America, this is your greatest hour. For I

have chosen you as the platform from which to launch the Good News of the Gospel into all the world. I have prospered you for such a time as this, putting My greatness into you. This is the appointed hour I have chosen for you to begin to rise up in the power of My Spirit and to fulfill all that I have foreordained for you," exhorts your Father.

The church of America will again stand tall before the world, even as the Statue of Liberty has stood tall and strong, raising high the flame of hope before the emigrants and the needy. Indeed, just as Lady Liberty was restored years ago, so now are God's people in America also under renovation and restoration. Yes, there is much, much change to come, but we must know that this time it is divine purpose that is at work. We must remember that the hand of our faithful Father is at work in this great hour, and we must yield to His touch and purposes as He prepares and equips us for our greatest challenge.

The Lord is again fanning the flame we once carried in our heart, America. He is again beginning to funnel the oil of His Spirit into our inner chambers, providing heavenly fuel for the flame of hope and passion that will again be lifted high by His last-day Church, even as the great torch is ever lifted toward Heaven by Lady Liberty. This flame of God's Spirit will never again be snuffed out by the powers that have withstood us. We must wake up, America, and arise as the wounded healer who will take the mantle of mercy and Good News to a dark and a dying world.

"I Am Calling You Up"

"Just as I heard the desperate cries and suffering of My people in Moses' day," says the Lord, "so have I seen, in this day, the suffering of those who have cried out to Me across this great land. Even as I called Moses up to the mountain to have an encounter with Me in the burning bush, so am I now calling you up, My beloved church of America, to My holy mountain. It is there where you will receive not only your deliverance, but also your commission to deliver the nations. Even as I called Peter, James and John up to the mountain of transfiguration to behold My glory, so am I now calling you up to the mountain of My presence to see the Son of Man glorified in this last day," says the Father.

"This is the day of My glory," says the Lord. "As you come into My glorious presence, you will be transformed. You will become My beautiful Bride, prepared and adorned for your Bridegroom, but you will also become an exceedingly great and fierce army prepared for the battle of the ages. You will be changed and glorified as you come up to the mountain of fire to fellowship with Me, your eternal Father. For My Body is now being cleansed, restored and shined up like a massive mirror that will finally begin to reflect the true character and nature of both the Lamb of God and of the Lion of the Tribe of Judah."

The Bride Will Be Mantled With Both Glory and Vengeance

"My beloved, wake up and *'arise, shine, for your light has come! And the glory of the Lord is risen upon you.'* [1] I am mantling My Bride in this hour," says the Lord, "with double glory."

Sarah, Abraham's bride, was so glorious that the king of Egypt was smitten with her beauty and sent his servants to fetch her, not knowing that she was Abraham's wife (see Genesis 12:11-20). And a second time, even in her advanced age, yet another king, Abimelech, was overcome with her glory (see Genesis 20).

"So will my Bride be in this hour," says the Lord, "mantled with double glory (even in her advanced age), causing the kings of this day to be drawn to her and to the brightness of her rising. [2] My glorious latter-day Bride will also be mantled with vengeance," says the Lord, "even as the prophet Elijah in his day."

Coming out of obscurity and stepping suddenly onto the pages of Israel's dark history, Elijah confronted the double trouble of the wicked duo, Ahab and Jezebel. *"Ahab did more to provoke the Lord God of Israel to anger than all the kings of Israel who were before him"* (1 Kings 16:33, NKJ). And as if his own sins were trivial, he married Jezebel, a Baal worshipper. But the deep darkness covering Israel was pierced and overcome by the anointing that had been reserved for just that very hour and purpose.

> "Even so," says the Lord, "have I also prepared the spirit of Elijah, Elisha and Jehu to confront and overcome the *'deep darkness'* that is now covering the earth. [3] This great double-portion anointing has been reserved according to My prophetic timetable, and is coming suddenly to confront and overcome, proclaiming *'the day of the vengeance of our God.'* [4] This anointing of vengeance will clear the way for the restoration of My people, and even prepare the way for My Son's return," [5] declares the Warrior-Father.

"I Am Avenging My Bride"

"Indeed, this is the hour of My vengeance toward the enemy," says the Lord, "for I am taking back My body and the rulership of My people. I am coming in great power to avenge My Bride, for I am truly a jealous God and a consuming fire. All that is not Me will be burned up, for I am weary of being misrepresented by the shepherds of the day, as they are motivated by their own gain and comfort.

"I am coming with great force and an avenging fire to run the false shepherds and hirelings out of My temple, even as My Son Jesus ran the money changers out of the Temple in His day. I am confronting the powers of religion, control, harlotry and witchcraft that have taken over My people. I will burn these powers of darkness from the roots up, [6] and they will never again have power over My people," says the Lord of Hosts.

"You will truly see the spirit of witchcraft cast down in this late hour," says the Lord. "The spirit of Elijah, Elisha and Jehu is pursuing it with a holy vengeance that has not yet been seen by My people. My Holy Ghost and fire missiles will pursue and utterly destroy it, including all its tentacles and barbs that have infiltrated and poisoned My people. This wicked spirit has violated, emasculated and neutralized even many of My choice servants, but I am coming now to destroy it as never before in history," promises the Lord.

"I have been waiting for this time, My people. I have been waiting for the hour of your vindication. And this is that very hour!" rejoices your Father. "I will restore all that the enemy has stolen from you, for your latter days will be more glorious than your former."

"I Am Making House Calls"

"Indeed, as you have sought Me and My presence, know that I am coming to you in this hour. I am coming first to the faithful and to My true leaders, to those who have, as the widow of Zarepheth, 'housed' the spirit of Elijah during the drought of My Spirit by sacrificing all for the sake of pleasing Me. [7] Now I am coming to you to repay and restore," says the Lord. "I have not seen your sacrifice as a small thing, and now I am sending you My double-portion resurrection power, even the very power of the greater works.

"This is the appointed hour for household restoration. Just as I raised up the widow's son by My Spirit that rested upon Elijah, [8] even so am I now sending you this same anointing, but in double measure, to deliver your households from the spiritual drought and also from the Ahabs of your day. I will be making house calls," promises the Lord, "to resurrect that which has died and to restore that which has been stolen."

*'Instead of your shame you shall have double honor,
And instead of confusion they shall rejoice in their portion.
Therefore in their land, they shall possess double;
Everlasting joy shall be theirs.'*   Isaiah 61:7, NKJ

"Even as My servant Job was restored double at the end of his suffering, so am I also restoring double to My faithful in this hour. Yes, I am coming to you, My faithful ones, for you will eat of the firstfruits of this new outpouring. As you are strengthened, and as you welcome this fiery anointing to fill every fiber of your being, you will then take My double-portion resurrection power into all the world, and beckon the people, as Noah, to come into the ark of My salvation. They will come in now because it is the season of ripeness and harvest. They will come in by the multitudes as never before. They will be drawn in by My Spirit, even as the animals were sovereignly drawn into the ark in Noah's day. I have prepared much, much room in the ark for them, so go to them now in My love and anointing," challenges the Father-of-all-the-earth.

The Master Welder Shapes Weapons of War

"The time is short, so you must take Me at My Word, and you must eat all of it that I give to you. For as both the fire of My Spirit and My Word are received together, they will bring life and transformation to your inner man, empowering you to become channels of the greater works that Jesus spoke of. [9] Some of My Word and Spirit will taste sweet, and some of it will taste bitter, as I complete the work of the cross in you. You must be conformed to My death before you can be an instrument of this double-portion resurrection power, otherwise you will be consumed in the fire that is to come. If you are living for yourself, you cannot live fully for Me. Allow Me to deliver you from reliance upon your flesh, so that you can be freed to fly as the eagles. Even My very own Son had to suffer before He could enter into His glory," [10] says the Father.

We must know that our Father will do this refining work in us, as we yield to Him. We must trust that it is not unto our destruction, but for our eternal benefit. The refiner's fire is necessary so that He can shape and weld us into His *"battle-ax[es] and weapons of war"* (Jeremiah 51:20, NKJ) for the end time. We must allow Him, as the Master Welder, to prepare us and weld us into swiftness, for we must run in haste as the hour is urgent. The harvest cannot wait, or it will be lost forever.

As we run at the Lord's bidding, in the power of His anointing and word, our very own feet will burn up the wicked, for they shall be ashes under the soles of our feet, as prophesied by the prophet Malachi (see 4:2). The Lord will give us strength and direction, just as He gave to His servant Joshua. He will empower us to take the land of promise — He *will* do it.

Time to Prepare, Noah-America

This is the hour of preparation, America, for the Lord is coming to you today even as He came to Noah in his day. Just as He told Noah to prepare and to build the ark for the saving of his household, so is He challenging and forewarning you today.

> "Just as I gave Noah specific instructions for the construction of the ark, so will I, in this hour, give to you very specific instructions for the building of this great latter-day ark," says the Divine Engineer. "Yes, this ark will accommodate your own family, but it will go far, far beyond that, to accommodate families from all tongues, tribes, peoples and nations of the earth."

> "Even as Noah and his family were saved by the ark he built to accommodate My purpose, so will you also be saved, My church of America, as you build to accommodate My vast latter-day purposes. As you give yourself to the building of the ark for My family, so will I also give Myself to the building of the ark for your family," promises your faithful Father.

Elijah: the Spirit of Preparation

God is sending the spirit of preparation, which is the spirit of Elijah, that was prophesied to come before the great and terrible day of the Lord, to work in us and through us for the preparation for His return (see Malachi 4:5).

We are entering the times that were foreseen by the prophets of old:

Yes, and all the prophets, from Samuel and those who follow, as many as have spoken, have also foretold these days. Acts 3:24, NKJ

They foretold of this season of:

                        4) The Return of Jesus (see Acts 3:19-21)
                3) The Restoration of all things
        2) Seasons of Refreshing
1) Repentance

The foundational stepping stone of repentance, followed by the next step up of refreshing, then the restoration of all things, will make the way for Jesus' return.

And that He may send Jesus Christ, who was preached to you before, whom heaven must receive [retain] until the times of restoration of all things, which God has spoken by the mouth of all His holy prophets since the world began. Acts 3:20-21, NKJ

The spirit of Elijah is restoring all things in order to prepare the way for the Bridegroom's return, just as John the Baptist prepared the way for Jesus long ago. John the Baptist went, *"before Him [Jesus] in the spirit and power of Elijah, 'to turn the hearts of the fathers to the children,' and the disobedient to the wisdom of the just, to make ready a people prepared for the Lord"* (Luke 1:17, NKJ).

"Yes, My Son Jesus is being retained in Heaven because the work of restoration has not yet been completed," says the Father. "Wake up, America, arise and receive this new outpouring of My spirit of restoration. Work with Me even as last-day Noahs to build the walls of marriages, families, cities and even whole nations, restoring all, all, all," [11] challenges the Lord of Hosts.

"All aboard, all A-B-O-A-R-D!"

"All aboard, all ab-o-ard!" cries the sovereign Conductor in this late hour. The train is now boarding, so run and buy your tickets quickly, for this is truly the great latter-day glory train. The great double engine is roaring and steaming with the firepower glory of the spirit of Elijah, and the prophetic wheels of time and eternity are just beginning to turn, so hurry while there is still time.

"Run to Calvary's bloody cross and freely purchase the gift of life My Son Jesus bought for all through the forgiveness of sins," pleads the loving Father. "Pay the ultimate price of complete surrender, losing your life, that you may find it forever."

The great Conductor of time and eternity is now calling in this late hour, "All aboard, all aboard!" We must not be as Esau, the brother of Jacob, who sold the blessing of his birthright for a single meal, weeping bitter tears afterward, forfeiting forever his one chance of blessing (see Genesis 25:30-34).

For you know that even afterwards, when he [Esau] desired to inherit the blessing, he was rejected, for he found no place for repentance, though he sought for it with tears. Hebrews 12:17

"The birth pangs and travail of the end have begun, My people," cries your heavenly Conductor-Father, "and there is no stopping them. The train is picking up speed now, so please come and board quickly, before it is too late.

"ALL AB-O-A-R-D!"

Endnotes:

1. Isaiah 60:1, NKJ.
2. See Isaiah 60:3.
3. Isaiah 60:2, NKJ.
4. Isaiah 61:2, NKJ.
5. See Matthew 17:11.
6. See Malachi 4:1.
7. See 1 Kings 17.
8. *Ibid.*
9. See John 14:12.
10. See Luke 24:26.
11. See Matthew 17:11.

Chapter 17

America's Mantle of Moses

American church, God has prepared and reserved a double-portion anointing, a latter-day mantle of Moses uniquely for you. Multitudes throughout the world are in valleys of decision and despair, desperately needing to see the rod of divine authority and power on their behalf. Not only do they need to hear, but they also need to see that God is a loving and merciful Father. They must understand that He is very concerned about their welfare. They need to see their heavenly Father vindicate them before their enemies, even as He vindicated the children of Israel before Pharaoh long ago through many signs and wonders.

"I am calling you up, America, I am calling you up!" cries your Founder-Father. "As you fellowship intimately with Me in the fiery glory of My presence, you will be launched into your destiny. There is no other way to discover and fulfill your mission in life, but to come up to the mountain to meet with Me. Some of you will encounter Me in anointed corporate meetings, and some of you will encounter Me privately, as Moses. Set your heart to seek Me, and keep seeking Me until you find Me.

"This is your hour to rise up and fulfill your destiny. This is the hour to come up to My holy mountain to be transformed, healed and delivered. You must get your eyes off yourself and your own comforts and get them back onto Me, your Founder and Father!

"My dear America, you have seen good times and bad times, but you must understand that this is your prophetic hour to wake up, for I am beginning to reveal Myself to many throughout this great land. This is the hour to forget yourself, search for Me with all your heart, turn aside from business as usual and listen to what I am saying. Know that, as you heed My word and go forth to bless others, you will find the deliverance and healing that you have been in such desperate need of. The hour is short. You must respond quickly, for the prophetic wheels of time and eternity are turning

America's Mantle of Moses

and the appointed hour of My deliverance has begun," exhorts your loving Father.

Double-Portion Signs and Wonders: the "Greater" Works

The Father is equipping His faithful servants with unprecedented power in these last days for the accomplishment of His purposes. Just as Pharaoh, the king of Egypt, would not let Israel go except under compulsion, so will it be in these last days also. Therefore, He is giving the power of His greater anointing that will begin to manifest in many miraculous signs and wonders, causing the yokes of bondage to be broken off masses of people so that they will be free to serve Him, the one and true living God.

"As My faithful servants respond in obedience to My beckoning in this hour," says the Lord, "I will mantle them with the rod of My authority in a way that has not been seen since the days of Moses. I will begin to do a greater work, the works that My Son spoke of, as I begin to touch and deliver not only communities and cities, but whole nations. I will truly stretch forth My mighty power, love and glory in this hour. As I turn up the heat of My anointing, you will begin to see the yokes of centuries of oppression and false religions destroyed," says the Lord of great power and might.

All Will Break Free!

In Moses' day, the Lord sent plague after plague over Egypt, slowly but surely loosening Pharaoh's hold on the Israelites. As Pharaoh's servants saw that Egypt was being destroyed, they counseled him to allow the men of Israel to be released. In Pharaoh's weariness, he sent for Moses and asked, "Who will be the ones who are going?" And Moses replied to him:

We will go with our young and with our old; with our sons and our daughters, with our flocks and our herds we will go.   Exodus 10:9, NKJ

Moses resolutely declared to the taskmaster Pharaoh that all of God's people would be delivered, and not only their people, but their wealth and possessions as well. As the people of God in this critical last day, let us now declare to our taskmaster Pharaohs, even to those who have withstood us for generations: "We will take all our people and all our possessions as we break free from centuries of slavery and bondage!" As latter-day Moseses, we proclaim, "We will all go free!" And as we break free, we will plunder our enemy-oppressors and take much spoil.

Wave after wave of anointing and deliverance is now bursting out of Heaven's river storehouse, having been reserved for such a time and purpose as this. Each wave of this anointing hits the enemy and loosens his hold on the people of God today, just as each plague in

America's Mantle of Moses

Moses' day hit Pharoah and loosened his hold on the children of Israel.

> "I will force the enemy to loose his hold," declares your Father-Deliverer, "so that all can go free, from the youngest in your households to the oldest. For I will have many from every tongue and tribe and nation of the earth who will praise and glorify Me in this late hour."

America's Appointed Day of Deliverance

We must realize that we have entered into the prophetic season of deliverance. For even before America was born, God knew the day of her deliverance. We will begin to see His hand stretched forth toward her enemies, even as the Lord stretched out His hand toward Egypt. We must understand that He is, and always has been, a God of timing. Even as the prophet Daniel proclaimed of Him:

> *Let the name of God be blessed forever and ever,*
> *For wisdom and power belong to Him,*
> *And it is He who changes the times and the epochs.*
> Daniel 2:20-21

"I am pouring out My anointing of deliverance in a fresh and more powerful way," says the Lord, "for many of My choice warriors are behind prison bars. I am coming in great wrath against the enemies that have oppressed them, for this is indeed the day of My vengeance" promises the Almighty. [1] "Just watch what I will do to your enemies!"

Needed: Double Agents

When the day of Israel's deliverance was at hand, God needed a man, an agent of deliverance, to accomplish all that He had promised. Every detail of Moses' life was carefully planned — his parents, the timing of his birth and his upbringing. He lived eighty years before he encountered the burning bush and first began to understand his destiny. However, God's hand had been upon him from the very beginning, as he was the chosen instrument of deliverance for Israel.

> "Even so, My dear ones, it was no accident that you were born during these final strategic days," says your Father. "Just as I planned the day of Israel's deliverance in Moses' day, so have I carefully planned every detail of the day of your deliverance, My people. I need many in this hour who will become agents of My double-portion delivering power. You have both the great honor and the weighty responsibility of becoming My latter-day Moseses.
>
> "Just as I instructed Moses and Aaron in what they were to do and to say, so will I instruct My faithful servants in this day, as they listen closely

to My voice. This mighty outpouring of My love and power will cause many in this hour to come to know Me as their Deliverer and Savior," says the Father-Lord.

"I am challenging you to put aside your personal plans and agendas, welcoming Me to indwell you yet more and more. This is the hour for you to decrease, so that I might increase within you, for the accomplishment of My latter-day purposes. Just as John the Baptist had to decrease as the Son of Man came forth, even so you must now decrease, My dear America, in preparation for My soon return.

"If you insist on walking in your own will and authority, know that you cannot carry My authority. I need courageous and obedient vessels in this hour who will allow Me to use them for My purposes. I desire to mantle them with the great rod of My authority, indeed with the latter-day mantle of Moses."

The Hour of Burning-Bush Encounters

Now Moses was pasturing the flock of Jethro his father-in-law, the priest of Midian; and he led the flock to the west side of the wilderness, and came to Horeb, the mountain of God. And the angel of the Lord appeared to him in a blazing fire from the midst of the

> *bush; and he looked, and behold, the bush was burning with fire, yet the bush was not consumed. So Moses said, "I must turn aside now, and see this marvelous sight, why the bush is not burned up."*
>
> *When the Lord saw that he turned aside to look, God called to him from the midst of the bush, "Moses, Moses!"*
>
> *And he said, "Here am I."* Exodus 3:1-4

This is truly the hour God is calling His many children aside for 'burning-bush encounters.' For, as Moses, we may quietly be going about our business one day, when we suddenly encounter His manifest presence.

Moses lived and grew for forty years in Pharaoh's palace, then served and matured in the desert for forty more years. But on the appointed day, he was called up to Mount Horeb, and there he was visited with the fire of God's presence. One hour he was tending sheep as he had done for forty years, and the next hour — suddenly — he was standing before the burning bush on holy ground, encountering the God of the whole earth, the great I AM THAT I AM!

> "You must pull aside with Me, for in the burning bush you will discover your destiny," says the Lord. "I have chosen this very day to begin revealing Myself to you, My beloved people. This is the hour of My fiery visitation.
>
> "My dear ones, for those who have eyes to see

and ears to hear in this hour, know that this is the appointed day I have chosen to call you up to My holy mountain," says the Father. "It is time, beloved, to begin to look up for those burning-bush encounters that I am bringing in this hour to call forth, transform and commission My people."

A New Thing

"Know that your many years of wilderness serving and waiting are quickly coming to an end, and the day of visitation and commissioning is upon you. As you are serving and seeking Me, know that I am drawing you up My holy mountain to encounter Me and My awesome fiery presence. Look with the eyes of your spirit in this hour, and listen closely as you hear Me call you aside by name, just as I called Moses. I may come to you in a way or at a time that you may not expect, so watch for Me with the eyes of your spirit. Remember My ways are not your ways, for I am doing a new thing in the earth!" celebrates the Lord.

As the people of God in this last day, we must understand that He cannot reveal Himself to us within the narrow limitations of religious traditions, for He is the great God of all the earth. He is the God of change, of surprises and of great diversity. We must listen and discern with the eyes of our heart and spirit, because if we try to find Him through our reasoning, we will most definitely miss Him. We must look for the fruit of liberty, restoration and abundant resurrection life. We must remember what the angels told the women the morning of the resurrection, as they were searching for Him in the tomb, *"Why do you seek the living One among the dead!"* (Luke 24:5).

Holy Ground

God is calling us aside in this hour because He wants to reveal Himself to us and because He wants to commission us for His purposes. He wants to reveal Himself to us in this strategic hour as the Holy God that He is. Did He not tell Moses to remove his sandals, for even the ground on which he was standing was holy? And has not God's holiness been profaned and misunderstood in this dark hour? Have not the so-called leaders of His Church lifted up their own standards before the people?

> "I am calling you out to consecrate and sanctify you in My fiery presence, so that you will be prepared to embrace and withstand My fiery purposes and challenges that lie ahead," explains your caring Father. "As you encounter Me in this hour, you must encounter My fire, for I am a consuming fire. As you fellowship with Me in

America's Mantle of Moses

spirit and in truth, you will fellowship with the fire of My holiness."

In these encounters, the Father will reveal to us greater understanding of who He is. We will come to know Him intimately and personally, as we must also invite Him to know us intimately and personally, bringing the searchlight of His Spirit into all our inward parts. We must welcome His loving light to dispel all darkness, fear and shame, all that would keep us away from Him.

We will come to know the Lord as the Source of our dreams and visions and as the God who fulfills all our heart's desires. Is He not the God who put compassion and love into Moses' heart on behalf of his brethren? Did He not cause Moses' heart to burn when he saw injustice and suffering? And did Moses not have to learn that he could do nothing in his own strength?

In the burning bush on Mount Horeb that day, He revealed to Moses what was on His heart:

I have surely seen the affliction of My people who are in Egypt, and have given heed to their cry because of their taskmasters, for I am aware of their sufferings. So I have come down to deliver them from the power of the Egyptians, and to bring them up from that land to a good and spacious land, to a land flowing with milk and honey....
Therefore, come now, and I will send you to Pharaoh,

so that you may bring My people, the sons of Israel, out of Egypt. Exodus 3:7-10

The Father: "I Am Concerned"

"Even as I heard the cries of the children of Israel long ago, so are the cries of many coming before Me in this hour, cries of great desperation rising throughout the land. I have seen and heard the sufferings of many who are oppressed by the wicked taskmasters of spiritual darkness and deceit. I hear the cries of children who are neglected, abused and orphaned. Daily I must hear the horrible silent screams of the many precious, innocent babies as they are murdered in the wombs of their own mothers. I hear the cries of women who are battered, broken and betrayed," says the Father.

"I see the confusion and futility of grown men who have lost their way and are entangled and oppressed by the harsh taskmasters of lust, addictions and the quest for materialism. I see the oppression of the gang members who feel they have to kill to be accepted by their peers. I feel the pain of the elderly who have been dishonored and forgotten, living out their lives in loneliness and poverty," says the Father. "I feel the silent aches of the poor, the homeless and the sick, and I see the great desperation of those who are bound by prison bars.

"I am also very concerned," says the loving Father of all, "about the harm that has been done to My people by the spirits of religion, legalism and witchcraft in the Church. I am concerned for My children who have been lulled to sleep, even as Samson in Delilah's lap, by mesmerizing and deceptive spirits that seek to destroy the anointing. I am very concerned about the multitudes in America that have been immunized against the true Gospel by the plastic counterfeit of religion.

"I need," says the Lord, "latter-day John the Baptists who will confront My people, again raising up the standard of My righteousness and holiness. I need latter-day Elijahs who will proclaim from the Mount Carmels and pulpits of America, *'If Baal be God, then serve him, but if God be God, then serve Him!'* I need latter-day Moseses who will go into the camp of religious leaders, to reveal the true and living One, Jesus, who is beginning to stand up and rule with the rod of loving authority over His Body," declares the Father.

Who Will Pull Aside?

Who will take the fire of the Good News to those who are oppressed, bringing deliverance through the anointing of the Word and Spirit together? Who will put aside daily affairs and agendas to come up to the mountain to fellowship with Him in the fire? Who will pay the price to take forth the rod of His authority in this final hour? And finally, who will carry the greater anointing that will begin to break the yokes of bondage that have oppressed and ruled many for centuries?

God is looking for those who will hunger and thirst for Him more than for life itself, and who will discipline and quiet themselves so they can hear that still, quiet voice that is beckoning in this strategic hour. He is looking for those who will leave the luxury and comfort of Pharaoh's court, forsaking the religious palaces that have been ruled by ambition and greed in this dark day, for the reproach of Christ. And He is looking for those who will draw aside to encounter that which is gloriously unfamiliar in the Holy Spirit.

> "Will *you* love Me enough to take My heart of compassion into the dark valleys of the broken, the hopeless and the needy?" asks the Father. "And will you diligently search for that burning bush of divine encounter, preparation and commissioning? And most importantly, will you make the lonely and sometimes difficult journey up the mountain of God to learn what is on My heart in this final hour?" invites the eager Father.

The Mantle of Meekness

Many are answering today as Moses did in his day: *"Who am I, that I should go"* (Exodus 3:11)?

"You must know," says your Father, "that I am choosing unlikely candidates in this hour, for I am choosing meek and humble vessels through which to show forth My glory into the whole earth. I am searching for vessels that have allowed and even welcomed My dealings, inviting Me to burn up the wood, hay and stubble of their lives. Did I not say that those who would be My disciples and follow Me must lay down their lives, taking up their crosses daily?"

Moses was the meekest man on the face of the earth (see Numbers 12:3). The Lord therefore trusted Moses to be faithful in His house. The Lord spoke to him face to face, even allowing him to see His form (see Numbers 12:7-8). Moses suffered the pain of being exiled from Egypt, leaving the familiar luxuries of his palace home and embracing the disciplines of shepherding in the wilderness for many years.

Month by month and year by year, meekness was worked into the fiber of his deepest heart and life. The Father had in mind from the beginning to prepare a choice vessel for the appointed day of deliverance, a vessel who would not take the glory unto himself. In the fierce and unrelenting heat of the desert, God shaped the heart of a man whom He could trust to be His representative in the earth, a man who would have His heart for the people.

"But before Moses could bear the weighty mantle of authority and responsibility for so many," says the Lord, "I first had to teach him to take My yoke and learn from Me meekness and lowliness of heart. [2] In Fatherly love and wisdom, I required that He first learn to become comfortable wearing the yoke of meekness before he could bear My glorious mantle of authority.

"I challenge you in this critical day, My latter-day Moseses, to receive My yoke of meekness:

" *'Have this attitude in yourselves which was also in Christ Jesus, who, although He existed in the form of God, did not regard equality with God a thing to be grasped, but emptied Himself, taking the form of a bond-servant, and being made in the likeness of men ... , He humbled Himself by becoming obedient to the point of death, even death on a cross. Therefore also God highly exalted Him, and bestowed on Him the name which is above every name.'* "
Philippians 2:5-9

Brokenness Releases the Anointing

Do you remember that the very costly, precious contents of Mary's alabaster box could not be released for

America's Mantle of Moses

the anointing of Jesus' head and feet that day long ago until it was broken? Do you understand that the broken box represented Mary's broken life? As she offered it to her King in worship, He redeemed and filled it with the rich fragrance of His love, glory and healing. And it became an eternal memorial, reminding all of Mary's lavish and unashamed adoration for the One she loved.

> "My dear ones," says your Father, "it is in the broken places that have been given to Me that I have chosen to shine through with the radiant light of My resurrection glory. Has it not always been so?"

If God places His glorious light inside a vessel that is complete and closed unto itself, who will benefit, other than the one vessel? But if He places His bright light inside a broken vessel, His radiant resurrection light will shine through every cracked and broken place, reaching far beyond that one vessel, bringing light to all those around. These meek and broken ones will then become beacons of light, even 'lighthouses' to those who live in this dark day. The brilliant light of the Sun of Righteousness is beginning to arise within them and through them in this new morning, burning off the haze of deep darkness that has covered the earth for much too long (see Malachi 4:2).

> "Am I not the God who exchanges weakness for glory?" asks the Lord of all.

...and God has chosen the weak things of the world to shame the things which are strong, and the base things of the world and the despised, God has chosen.
1 Corinthians 1:27-28

"I allowed even the precious body of My only Son Jesus to be broken on the cross, so that His glorious resurrection life could burst forth three days later. And do you understand that He is the firstborn Son of many who are now following His example, also finding their way to glory by the way of the cross?"

Multiplied in the Lord's Hands

Do not be deceived into thinking that you have too little to offer to the Lord. Remember the mother who unknowingly fed the multitudes that were following Jesus by preparing but one lunch of loaves and fishes for her small son. As the boy gave that one lunch to Jesus, it was multiplied again and again in the hands of the Master, feeding thousands. One mother provided for her one son, who in turn provided for the multitudes by giving to Jesus.

And is Jesus not the Living Bread Himself who came down out of Heaven to be broken and multiplied in the hands of His Father? His grace and salvation are continuing to be freely offered to all those who will partake of Him, indeed to all those who hunger for eternal life in this last day.

And what about the widow who had only two mites? Did Jesus not teach those around that day that she had given more than the wealthy who gave much out of their abundance? By her example, how much has this dear woman taught of heavenly principles to all who have read the Scriptures (see Mark 12:42-44). Her giving continues and continues.

> "Am I not the One who created all that you see out of nothing, and am I not the God who took the dust of the earth and fashioned man in My own image? You must understand that I delight in taking your lives, My dear ones, no matter how meager and broken they seem to you. For I will show forth the greatness of My love toward you, and also the greatness of My love for others through you. Is this not the heart of My message from Calvary?"

It Is Time to Arise and Shine

> "It is in your deficiencies and broken places, My people," says the Lord, "that the King of Glory wants to manifest His all sufficiency, healing and deliverance, not only *to you*, but *through you*, for many, many others. Your lives are to be living epistles and testimonies, to be read by those who do not know there is a living God who is good and whose name is Jesus.

"Are you not My Bride, the one I've chosen to glorify? My brilliant latter-day light is now beginning to shine through you, as the light of many suns. For the Light of the World Himself has taken up residence within you in this dark day. As you offer up your lives, My children, know that I will surely take them. Just as a light bulb is screwed into a socket, I will graft you into the socket of Calvary's cross, so that you will become both a receiver and a transmitter of all the light and resurrection power of Jesus Himself," promises your Father.

Arise, shine, for your light has come,
And the glory of the Lord has risen upon you.
For behold, darkness will cover the earth,
And deep darkness the peoples;
But the Lord will rise upon you,
And His glory will appear upon you.
And nations will come to your light,
And kings to the brightness of your rising.

Isaiah 60:1-3

"I Will Equip You"

We must understand that all God needs from us is our willingness. For this is not about who we are or what we can do. He will give to us all that we have need of to accomplish His latter-day purposes, just as He gave to a Hebrew shepherd named Moses so many years ago, all that was needed to force Pharaoh, the king of Egypt, to release the children of Israel.

> "As I commissioned Moses from the burning bush of Mount Horeb," says the Lord, "I gave to him everything he would need:
>
> - **My Passion**: *"I have surely seen the oppression of My people who are in Egypt, and have heard their cry because of their taskmasters, for I know their sorrows. So I have come down to deliver them."*
> - **My Purpose**: *"I will send you ... that you may bring My people ... out ... ."*
> - **My Promise/Presence**: *"I will certainly be with you."*
> - **My Power**: *"I will stretch out My hand, and strike Egypt with all My wonders."*
> - **My Provision**: *"I will give this people favor ... . When you go, you shall not go empty-handed ... . [You shall go with] articles of silver, articles of gold and clothing ... . You shall plunder the Egyptians."*
> - **My Prophetic Voice**: *"I will be with your mouth and teach you what you shall say."* [3]

Does not the master of the house supply his servants with everything needed for his estate? And does not a caring father supply his children with everything they have need of to be blessed and to accomplish their tasks? Has God not always been our faithful Father-Provider?

"I supplied Adam and Eve with sunshine and air, a beautiful garden to eat from and animals to name and have dominion over," reminisces your Father. "I gave them one to another to love and to bear children. And when I commissioned Noah to build the ark, I supplied everything he needed: the gopher wood, the pitch, his sons-in-law to help, strength for the task and very specific instructions. In all the history of My people, I have *never* failed to supply what was needed to accomplish My purposes."

Silver and Gold

As God begins to pour out this greater anointing of deliverance, the strongholds of the enemy will be plundered, even as Egypt was plundered long ago. As yokes of bondage and oppression are broken, the enemy will be forced to release his hold on the wealth that belongs to God's people. The children of Israel had lived in slavery and poverty for four hundred and thirty years, but when God brought them out, He brought them out *"with silver and gold"* (Psalm 105:37).

"Yes, you will plunder the wealth of the wicked as at no other time in history, for I have purpose in this hour," says the Lord on high. "Just as I supplied Moses and the children of Israel with the wealth and resources necessary for the building of the Tabernacle in their day, so will I supply you with all that is needed. I will supply all the resources needed to build the largest soul-winning ark of all the ages. I will supply My Bride with all the necessary resources of preparation and beautification, and I will supply My beloved Israel with everything that is required to be completely and gloriously restored.

"I am opening the storehouses of Heaven in this late hour, My people, because it is time to be about My work. I will now begin to funnel the wealth and lavishness of Heaven itself through My choice servants. I am pouring out an anointing of provision upon those who, like Solomon of old, desire to serve and govern My people in the spirit of justice, meekness and wisdom. My servant Solomon was blessed because it pleased Me that he did not seek for himself riches, but rather he had a heart to serve My people. [4] And I was able to trust Moses with great wealth and authority because, *'when he had grown up, [he] refused to be called the son of Pharaoh's daughter ... considering the reproach of Christ greater riches than the treasures of Egypt.'* " [5]

A Last-Day Tabernacle Will Be Built

Our faithful Father lavishly provided for the building of the Temple in Solomon's day, a temple which was but a foreshadowing of things to come. How much more will He provide for the building of that eternal temple, the city that Abraham was seeking, *"the city which has foundations, whose architect and builder is God"* (Hebrews 11:10)? And could this be the same city and tabernacle that John saw when he was on the Island of Patmos many years later?

> *I saw the holy city, new Jerusalem, coming down out of heaven from God, made ready as a bride adorned for her husband.*
> *And I heard a loud voice from the throne, saying, "Behold, the tabernacle of God is among men, and He shall dwell among them, and they shall be His people, and God Himself shall be among them."*
>
> Revelation 21:2-3

"My dear America, you must recall how the children of Israel plundered Egypt as a result of My delivering power, enabling the Israelites to build the Tabernacle in the wilderness to worship Me," says your generous Father. "And so will you now plunder *your* enemies, enabling you to build that eternal tabernacle-ark, the temple whose latter glory will be greater than all."

Prophetic Mouthpieces

"Just as I promised to be with Moses' and Aaron's mouths, telling them what to say, so will I be with you today. The world and even My people have been confused and wearied from the many voices that were supposedly speaking on My behalf. I am able to speak for Myself; I need willing and obedient vessels who will allow Me to speak through them. I am weary of the man-pleasing and compromising spirits that have caused My people to be lukewarm. I am looking for vessels who will be consumed with My burning passions, speaking and displaying My true heart," says the Father.

"Learn from the prophets of old, My latter-day people. I am beginning to raise up true prophetic voices who are speaking clearly what is on My mind and heart in this hour. Listen to them, for in My voice you will find guidance for the hour, protection and even life itself. There are many voices in America promoting self-agendas, but you must forsake them, take up your cross, and follow Me.

"I am a God of simplicity and clarity, My people. Did I not say that the Gospel was simple enough for babes to understand and receive? My true voices are simple, clear and specific," cautions your Father. "They always lift up the name of Jesus and honor the work of the cross. They always honor My infallible Word and the moving of My precious Holy Spirit.

"Indeed, I will bring forth present-day Aarons who will be the mouthpieces alongside present-day Moseses. I will be with your mouth," says the Lord who made the mouth. "Look to Me to find out who your Aarons are. They may not be those you thought I would have chosen. You must look to Me for everything in this strategic hour of battle and harvest."

We must remind ourselves that God's true prophetic voices will speak not only pleasant things. Rather, they will speak His truth, the truth that will set many free. We must not look for personalities, but instead look and listen for His truth and life-voice. Although we may or may not like the personality and style of His prophets, we must honor them and honor His Word that He is bringing through them for the deliverance of His people.

Mothers and Fathers Speak Truth

The wise and loving Father of all is preparing His beloved children for the greatest challenges and the greatest battle of all time. Does not an earthly father instruct, train and even admonish his children, in order to equip them for the challenges of life? In anticipation of a great war, is it not the wise and caring general who presses his troops to the maximum, training them for the rigors of the battlefield ahead and preparing them, not just for survival, but for victory?

The Father-General is now raising up mothers and fathers who will speak His truth for the purpose of maturing and preparing the Body for the great battle ahead. We must put aside milk and diapers *"and grow up into Him who is the Head."* This battlefield is only for those who are spiritually strong and developed. It is time to go into the gyms of daily life to exercise God's truths and to develop strength and stamina. We cannot wait until the heat of the great battle to begin exercising and learning the weapons of our warfare, for it will be too late, and we will be overcome. His voice to the Body in this hour is the voice of preparation, of instruction and exhortation, and of loving admonishment.

> "The time is short," warns the Father-General, "and there is much to learn and overcome in order to be ready for what lies ahead."

The Rod of Authority

The God of the heavens and the earth has an urgent latter-day purpose. The appointed day of deliverance has arrived, and many latter-day Moseses are needed to take the rod of authority to deliver the nations.

Just as God manifested the rod of His authority and power through Moses, so will He also manifest Himself in this day through His faithful sons and daughters.

As we stand as His representatives, we must remember to stand in His name and authority rather than in our own. When Moses stood before Pharaoh, he did not stand in his own authority: *"The Lord God of the Hebrews has sent me to you"* (Exodus 7:16).

> "I will anoint you with the rod of My authority, as you humbly and obediently follow My instructions. The rod of authority will be a shepherd's rod, because I will mantle only those who have received My love for the sheep," says the caring Father-Shepherd. "I am looking for those who will represent Me accurately in this hour. I am looking for those who have become empty in themselves, but full in Me, that they would reflect My heart of love and mercy toward the peoples of the earth, while at the same time executing My vengeance toward My enemies."

The Commander of Armies Is Now Dispatching Troops

> "As you fellowship with Me in My fiery presence on the holy mountain, I will speak to you personally about the things that are on My heart, revealing to you your specific role and mission in this latter-day battle. I will speak to you about where and how you are to serve Me in this critical hour. You will come to know Me as the Commander of Armies, even as Joshua knew Me, for I am now dispatching troops to the ends of the earth and positioning them strategically to

bring about great deliverance, salvation and victory.

"I am becoming more specific in this hour of commissioning," says the Lord. "Even as I sent Moses to Egypt to deliver the children of Israel, so am I now sending many servants into all the nations of the world to bring about great deliverance. I am commissioning you to deliver My many children from their oppressive taskmasters in this dark day."

Launched Like Rockets

"Come to Me, My dear children. Let My eternal fire burn deeply within you, and receive your marching orders," challenges the Captain of the Hosts of the Lord. "I will commission you out of the fire, even as I did My servant Moses in his day."

We must come up the mountain of God and bask in the burning bush of His fiery presence. As we do, one day (known only to Him), we will be shot up like a fiery rocket into realms of destiny and glory that we know not of! Many of us are now in the final countdown stages just before lift-off. It is imperative that we abide continually on the launchpad of God's presence, keeping our radio-focus tuned only to the Commander's voice.

We must keep ourselves strapped into the heart of His will by continuing to consecrate ourselves wholeheartedly. We must trust His timing, knowing that as we yield to Him, no matter what things look like now, He is working out His strategic purposes in our lives.

The Divine Chess Master Orchestrates Triumph

The Father is as the brilliant chess master who has already won the game, but must wait patiently for each turn to be taken. He must wait for each piece to be moved and removed, so that at just the right time the victory will become evident. The peoples of the earth are like players in a great chess match between the powers of light and darkness, good and evil. The sacrifice of Jesus on the cross was the strategic winning play of the game. The Father has allowed the enemy to overplay his hand, so that in the fullness of time, He would use him even as He used Pharaoh in Moses' day, to show forth His triumph.

We must allow God to position us strategically, even as the chess master positions his pieces, so that each of us can, in turn, systematically do our part to bring about victory. We must trust the Lord's moving and leadings, for He alone can see the entire chess board from Heaven's perspective, therefore He alone has true perspective. As His children, we must know that He is orchestrating all things in great wisdom and lovingkindness.

"Some of you will be removed from your homes and familiar surroundings to be repositioned into other communities, cities and even other countries," says the faithful Chess Master. "Some of you will be plucked out of your current vocations, being repositioned into new business ventures that I create. Some who are involved in commerce will find themselves also in ministry. Some of you already in ministry will suddenly find yourselves operating in new functions and greater giftings. You must trust Me completely and implicitly in this critical hour, My dear ones, to position you into the place that will enable you to fulfill your highest destiny.

"It is difficult for you to imagine just how very much is at stake, for so many, many precious souls are hanging in the balance. There is much preparation work to be done: the Bride to be matured and adorned and Israel to be restored to her homeland and to her Messiah. You must work, My children, while it is still *'day'* (John 9:4). Again, I challenge you to trust Me as your Father-Chess Master to reposition you so that you can fulfill your highest destiny and function."

Endnotes:

1. See Isaiah 61:2.
2. See Matthew 11:29.
3. Exodus 3:7-4:12, NKJ.
4. See 1 Kings 3:5-13.
5. Hebrews 11:24-26.

Chapter 18

The Great Eagle Shall Rise Again

The American church has dwelt in the dry wilderness places, tending but a few sheep, even as Moses, for such a very long time now. She has been publicly reproached again and again, but God has known from the beginning, even as He did with Moses, that she would be a chosen vessel of deliverance for these last days. Her reproach and shame will very soon be turned into honor, glory and victory.

The American church is being delivered from reliance upon herself, and she is growing in meekness and wisdom so that she will be able to carry the weighty mantle of authority and glory that was prepared and reserved for her from long ago.

America Forgot

For a season, the American church forgot who she

was, but God is reminding her of her true identity and destiny in this late hour. Remember King Nebuchadnezzar of old, who went through a season of humiliation because of his pride. For a season he was made to dwell among the base things of the earth, even among the animals, losing his reason and identity. But when that season was over, King Nebuchadnezzar lifted up his eyes to Heaven, came to himself and glorified God:

> *I ... lifted up my eyes to heaven, and my understanding returned to me; and I blessed the Most High and praised and honored Him who lives forever:*
>
> *For His dominion is an everlasting dominion,*
> *And His kingdom is from generation to generation.*
> *All the inhabitants of the earth are reputed as nothing;*
> *He does according to His will in the army of heaven,*
> *And among the inhabitants of the earth.*
> *No one can restrain His hand*
> *Or say to Him, "What have You done?"*
>
> Daniel 4:34-35, NKJ

"It is time now, My American church," says your Father-Founder, "to again lift up your eyes toward Heaven, so that your spiritual understanding, reasoning and true identity will return. I never called you to be your own ruler in My Kingdom, but instead, I called you to be My humble and obedient representative to the nations. Yes, you are a great nation, America, but did you forget that it was I who created you with the breath of My mouth, imparting My very own life and greatness into you? You must never again take My glory for yourself, for I am, indeed, a jealous God and a consuming fire.

"You must be very careful to bear the ark of My presence in accordance with My instructions and in humility. Otherwise, you will find yourself cast aside as Uzzah, who presumptuously sought to steady the ark in David's day and perished. [1] You must remind yourself that, apart from Me, you can do nothing, [2] for you were created by Me, even as the moon that reflects the glory of the sun. Yes, you are My beloved and cherished sons and daughters, kings and priests, a glorious Bride, and heirs of salvation, but you must always, always give honor only to the Lamb-Bridegroom, and to His wishes and plans."

The Enemy Seeks to Kill America's Children

The enemy is so terrified of America's destiny that he is trying very desperately and franticly to destroy her from the inside out, especially attacking her children. The enemy slaughtered many babies in the day of Moses because he realized through prophecy that it was the appointed time for a deliverer to be born. And in this day, he has slaughtered many through abortion and through gang violence and drugs, because he understands once again that it is the appointed time of deliverance. The hosts of darkness tremble, knowing that a generation is coming forth with the Moses mantle, preparing the way for Messiah's return.

> "I am looking," says the Lord, "for valiant warrior-fathers and mothers who will protect the younger generation of prophets and apostles I am bringing forth. I need courageous and mature warriors who are willing to lay down their lives for My anointed ones. I need proven and veteran warriors who will place themselves between My children and the wicked enemies of religion, antichrist and witchcraft that seek their destruction.

> "And I am looking," says the Lord, "for those in this day who will cover My infant-purposes, like Moses' mother and father covered him, hiding him from the Pharaoh's death edict. Be comforted, My latter-day mothers and fathers, in knowing that My wisdom and instruction will be with you as you cover My infant-purposes, even as I was with Moses' parents as they hid the infant-deliverer from Pharaoh. I will send the very hosts of Heaven itself to guide, protect and provide for you in this critical hour, My courageous ones.

"Be assured that the enemy will not prevail against you, My latter-day warriors. Again, I declare to you, he will not prevail, as I have foreordained this very hour to be the hour of your deliverance and commissioning. The enemy cannot and will not stop My eternal plan," promises your Father.

America's New Name of Destiny, The Great Eagle

Yes, America, you have been battered and beaten by many storms, and you have been parched and dry for a very long time indeed, but know that this is a new day, and everything you've gone through will now serve you in this critical last-day battle. It's true that you've been scarred in your battles, but does not your Master also bear the victory scars of Calvary? And did not your brother Paul also bear upon his own body many scars from whippings, stoning, snakebite and shipwreck?

"Do not focus upon your wounds, lacks or your past reproach and trials," exhorts your Father, "but rather focus upon Me and upon your glorious future. It matters not that you are scarred, My American church, or that you walk with a limp as My servant Jacob, while you have sought Me through your long, dark night of wrestling. What matters is that you focus on Me in this new day, receiving your new name of destiny, My Great Eagle."

It was indeed no accident that the eagle was chosen as America's national symbol. For from the very beginning, even before she was discovered, the Father knew that it would be America who would carry the weighty last-day mantle of His authority and mercy to the nations. Even as He built character, majesty and strength into the eagle, so has He built it into you, America, into your very foundation and cornerstone. Know that no man, nor any power of Hell itself, can undo, or steal, what God has done in you. For you were truly built upon the rock, upon the Rock of Ages Himself, through His Spirit that motivated your founding fathers.

Take courage now, dear ones, and begin to spread and exercise your wings, for the winds of His Spirit are beginning to blow again across this great land. Be strong once again in Him, and in the power of His might.

"Yes, I hear your cries, America, and I am on My way," promises your Father-Founder. "This is truly your hour of destiny, the very purpose for which you were founded, protected and developed."

Stretch Forth Your Wings

Great Eagle, it is time for you to stretch forth those majestic wings of destiny once again, from sea to shin-

The Great Eagle Shall Rise Again

ing sea. You were created to soar into the heights of God's Spirit and glory in this late hour. He created you to extend your great wings of strength and mercy over the whole earth, catching the powerful last-day wind currents that will take you into the fulfillment of your destiny.

Dear old Eagle, your joints, shoulders and muscles have become stiff and even atrophied from so many years of ease. But are you not awakening morning by morning to the fresh, warm oil that He is now pouring out upon those joints and muscles? Are you not aware of the soothing, heavenly lubrication of His Spirit that has been reserved for this prophetic purpose and for this very hour?

Surely you are sensing the hand of the Father as He lovingly touches your great shoulders, administering the strengthening virtue of Calvary through the healing balm of His Spirit. As you begin to rotate and stretch those great shoulders, are you not sensing renewed life and vigor? Dear old Eagle, know that God is indeed renewing your youth, as many of His faithful ones have waited on Him for a very long time.

Your Best Days Are Ahead

> "Your best days are ahead, My dear Eagle-America," promises your Father. "Don't look back, for truly your best days are ahead."

It is time now to rouse from the slumber of your

nest to sense the latter-day wind currents that are beginning to blow, hovering high over America, in double portion. The Father did not design and create you to dwell in your own comfort nests.

"I created you to catch My Spirit-currents," says your Father, "causing you to fellowship with Me, flying high over the glorious mountains of the earth, but also going with Me into the desperate valleys, where every tribe and tongue of people dwell. For such a time as this, My dear Eagle, I have prepared and reserved you from long ago.

"Rise up, America, for I, as the Father of All and the Captain of Armies, will fly with you into your destiny, causing you to accomplish all that I have foreordained for you from the beginning of time.

"You must turn toward Me, My beloved Eagle, and stretch forth the wings of your faith, trusting in Me as your Father-Founder once again. As you do, you will experience the lifting of My Spirit that will bear you up high above both the carnality of your past, and the wicked latter-day forces that seek your destruction."

The Eagle Will Endure Last-Day Storms

"Yes, it is true that the very gates of Hell are now battering against you yet again and again with great ferocity, even as terrific hurricane winds

The Great Eagle Shall Rise Again

and waves batter the coastline, but know that they will not prevail against you, My people. You must continually learn to hide yourself in Me, and in My latter-day purposes, rather than in your own agendas, for that is what has made you vulnerable to the enemy's attack again and again.

"As you learn to truly hide yourself in Me, you will discover that I will take the batterings and beatings that Hell is spewing forth with such great latter-day intensity. Humble yourselves, and crawl under the shelter of My strong, eternal wings, and hide yourself in that secret place of intimate fellowship with Me, where the enemy cannot harm you," exhorts your loving Father.

As you remain under the Father's wings, under the very shadow of the Almighty Himself, you will be protected. As He moves you must also move with Him, even as the children of Israel, who followed the cloud by day and the pillar of fire by night. Please, please do not wander from His covering of protection and glory. Even as a faithful hen covers and protects her young brood, so is the Lord covering and protecting you in this late hour. You must stay close to Him, under His Lordship and covering, for there are indeed wicked forces that seek your destruction. You must not become too comfortable, for God is moving suddenly and frequently in this critical hour of preparation, so you must be prepared to move quickly with Him.

The Sun of Righteousness Himself Indwells the Eagle

Allow the Sun of Righteousness Himself to cover you in this prophetic hour, dear Eagle, with His strong healing wings. As you are growing in meekness, know that He is arising within you in this late hour (see Malachi 4:2), indwelling you yet more and more. Know that as you decrease, He is increasing within you, for He is replacing your own heart for yourself with His heart for the nations.

His double anointing is filling your wings with mercy and restoration for His people on the one side, and with a fierce vengeance toward enemy forces on the other side. Indeed, it is the Sun of Righteousness Himself who is now beginning to come forth within you, stretching out His own healing, delivering wings within yours, dear Eagle. As you continue to lose the ambition of your self-life, know that His resurrection power will continue to increase, so that even the greater works that Jesus spoke of will begin to be manifest through you, delivering many.

> "You will become My vehicle through which I will fly to all the peoples of the earth," explains the Father, "bringing deliverance, salvation and restoration, preparing the way for My Son's re-

turn. You must give all the glory and honor to Me, as I work through you for the accomplishing of My latter-day purposes, remembering that you are but a steward, as Moses was, of My Kingdom.

"We will fly together, yoked on the one side with meekness and humility, and on the other side with glorious power and might. As you become yoked with Me, flying into the heights of My Spirit, you will begin to see through My own eyes, from Heaven's eternal perspective. It is there where you will finally begin to understand who you are and the divine purpose for which you were born.

"We will fly together, My Great Eagle, on the latter-day winds of destiny!" rejoices your Father.

You Will Succeed, America

It is imperative that you follow the Lamb-Lion wherever He goes in this critical hour, obeying Him as your Commanding General not only when you understand, but even when you do not. You must follow Him not only when you feel good and rested, but also when you are battle-worn and weary, for the time of preparation is shorter than you realize. Remember, you will be able to stand in this rigorous and challenging latter day only in the Lord's strength that has been deposited within you from the very beginning.

> "Know that you will succeed in that which I have called you to, My Eagle-America, because you were birthed out of My father's heart of love for the nations. You and your great wings were carefully formed and tailored for the prophetic purpose of touching all the peoples of the earth with My love, mercy and glory, lifting high the name above all names, the name of My precious Son Jesus. And yes, multitudes upon multitudes will be drawn to Him, into the latter-day ark of salvation that is now under construction, My great Eagle-Noah."

The Warrior-Eagle Makes a Resolution

America, you must resolve to seek your Father as never before. You must resolve to grasp Him even as the warrior-Eleazar, of King David's three mighty men. This mighty warrior stood alone, defying the entire Philistine army that had gathered for battle, while the men of Israel retreated. Alone and in his weariness, he continued to stand against all odds. He grasped his sword, until his hand stuck to it:

> *He [Eleazar] arose and attacked the Philistines until his hand was weary, and his hand stuck to the sword.*

> *The Lord brought about a great victory that day; and the people returned after him only to plunder.*
> 2 Samuel 23:10, NKJ

It is imperative that you grasp Him, Warrior-Eagle, as Eleazar grasped his sword. You must grasp His Word, His anointing, and even His very own heart in this late hour, until you are 'stuck' to them, becoming one with them.

"Even as I used Eleazar to stand against many, bringing about a great victory for Israel," says the Lord, "so will I use you in this late day, My courageous Warrior-Eagle. You will indeed stand against the very hordes of Hell itself to bring about great last-day victory as I manifest the triumph of Calvary through you."

New Winds Are Blowing

You've been in your nest much too long, Great Eagle, for do you not long to soar into the heights of God's glory for which you were created? Have you not become restless and weary of arranging and rearranging your own nest yet again and again? Do you not long to breathe the clean, invigorating air high above the stifling carnality that you've dwelled in for so very long?

It is imperative, dear ones, that you escape the choking smog of your own expirations, yearning instead for that sweet, eternal life-breath that proceeds from the heavenly throne. For you are just beginning to sense the powerful wind currents as they are building, swelling and even swirling with great intensity over strategic churches, communities and cities across this great land. Surely you are longing to see the earth and the peoples therein from Heaven's perspective, even as the Father does.

> "Come, My beloved Eagle-America. Come and fly with Me," invites the Lord on high. "Come and catch the fresh, new double winds of deliverance and restoration that are just beginning to blow over the whole earth.
>
> "Even as I blew into Adam's nostrils the breath of life in the beginning, so am I now, as the Father of all, again blowing My eternal life-breath deeply into the hearts of men in this late hour. As I commanded My servant Ezekiel to prophesy to the dead bones in the midst of the valley, so am I now commanding life into the dead bones of the valleys of America in this urgent hour:
>
> " *'O dry bones, hear the word of the Lord!*
> *Thus says the Lord God to these bones: "Surely I will*
> *cause breath to enter into you, and you shall live.*
> *"Come from the four winds, Oh breath, and breathe*
> *on these slain, that they may live." ' "*
> Ezekiel 37:4-5 and 9, NKJ

The Great Eagle Shall Rise Again

The Spirit of Elijah Will Resurrect the Eagle

Beloved Eagle-America, allow the Lord of Glory once again to be intimate with you, to overshadow you and to blow His eternal life-breath deeply into you. He will resurrect you, even as He resurrected the son of the widow of Zarepheth and the son of the Shunamite woman. Even as He sent His prophets to them, so is He now sending His spirit of Elijah/Elisha, His prophetic spirit of restoration, to resurrect that which has died within you.

Both these prophets stretched themselves out, laying their own bodies upon the bodies of the dead sons as they prayed. Even so, the Lord is now stretching Himself out upon that which is dead within you, Eagle-America, laying His Spirit of resurrection upon you, breathing His very own life-breath into you once again, until you are warmed and restored. Yes, He did lay His presence upon you in the beginning when He conceived and formed you, but know that He is now coming to you *a second time*.

> "I hear the cries of My faithful children across this land welcoming Me in this day," says your Father, "even as the widow and the Shunamite who welcomed Me into their homes long ago. This is truly your appointed day to rise again, My beloved Eagle-America," commands your Father.

Has the Lord not explained that Elijah must indeed come first, restoring all things before His return (see Matthew 17:11)? And did He not explain that seasons of refreshing would follow repentance, and that the restoration of all things must precede His return (see Acts 3:19-21)? Did the prophet Malachi not prophesy that He would send Elijah to restore before the great and terrible day of the Lord (see Malachi 4:5)? Who can argue that America has now entered into the day of fire that Malachi saw from afar (see Malachi 4:1), ushering in the spirit of Elijah, which is the spirit of restoration?

You Will Live Again, Eagle-America!

"You will live again, My beloved Eagle," promises your Father. "Your heart will beat again with the fervor and the passion of your first love toward Me. You will rise up, stretching and exercising your great wings, again catching the winds of My Spirit and purpose, becoming airborne. As you fellowship with Me in the heights of My Spirit, your eyes will again become clear as you 'come to yourself,' remembering who you are and for what great purpose you were conceived.

"You will be strengthened," promises your faithful Father. "You will endure and overcome, accomplishing all that I have foreordained for you from the very beginning.

The Great Eagle Shall Rise Again

"Long ago, my servant Joel prophesied last-day restoration:

" 'Then I will make up to you for the years
That the swarming locust has eaten,
The creeping locust, the stripping locust, and the gnawing locust,
My great army which I sent among you.'

Joel 2:25

" 'And it shall come to pass afterward
That I will pour out My Spirit on all flesh;
Your sons and your daughters shall prophesy,
Your old men shall dream dreams,
Your young men shall see visions;
And also on My menservants and on My maidservants
I will pour out My Spirit in those days.'

Joel 2:28-29, NKJ

"Receive My resurrection life-breath even now, My beloved Eagle, for your latter days will be much more glorious than your former. It is time now to hoist up your welcome banners toward Heaven, beseeching My precious Holy Spirit to invade your deepest hearts, lives and families. Welcome My eternal life-breath into all that has been dead to Me, and you will receive My resurrection power. Rejoice, for your hour of deliverance, vindication and commissioning has come. Rejoice, America, for your restoration is truly at hand!"

Endnotes:

1. See 2 Samuel 6:6-7.
2. See John 15:5.

For information about our ministry, visit out web site:

www.mantlesofglory.org

Contact us through our e-address:

karla@mantlesofglory.org